WASHINGTON

KNOW YOUR STATE

ACTIVITY BOOK

THIS BOOK BELONGS TO:

Manufactured in Versaille, Kentucky, in April, 2015, by Quad/Graphics

First Edition
19 18 17 16 15   5 4 3 2 1

Published by
Gibbs Smith
P.O. Box 667
Layton, Utah 84041

1.800.835.4993 orders
www.gibbs-smith.com

Designed by Nate Padavick
Edited by Michelle Branson
Production and design assistance by Virginia Snow
Printed and bound in the United States
Gibbs Smith books are printed on either recycled, 100% post-consumer waste, FSC-certified papers or on paper produced from sustainable PEFC-certified forest/controlled wood source. Learn more at www.pefc.org.

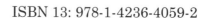

ISBN 13: 978-1-4236-4059-2

WASHINGTON

KNOW YOUR STATE

ACTIVITY BOOK

Megan Hansen Moench

GIBBS SMITH
TO ENRICH AND INSPIRE HUMANKIND

Greetings, Washingtonians! I'd like to welcome you as you begin your journey to learn more about the great state of Washington. You are so lucky to live in such a beautiful place where Mother Nature has been hard at work for years and years creating unbelievable landscapes! As an educator, I know just how fun it can be for kids to learn about Washington's snow-capped purple mountains, rolling hills on farmland, busy coastal cities, wooded green mountainsides, mysteries of ancient people, lifestyles of mountain men, expeditions of early explorers, and so much more!

In this book, you will learn more about the land, people, places, and science of Washington while practicing core skills. But, more importantly, you will have fun learning about the unique traits of this beautiful, wonderful, magnificent, incredible, great state of Washington!

Turn the page to begin your adventure!

CONTENTS

7 VOCABULARY

71 GEOGRAPHY & SOCIAL STUDIES

129 READING & WRITING

187 SCIENCE

229 MATH

254 STATE SYMBOLS

256 GLOSSARY

262 ANSWER KEY

VOCABULARY

8   How to Use a Dictionary or Glossary

10   Find the Hidden Message!

11   Field Trip: A Day at the Museum

12   Many Kinds of History

13   My Artifact

14   Tools of History

15   Fill in the Blank

16   Where in the World Are We?

18   The Land We Call Home

20   Hike The Maze

21   Snapshots of Washington

22   Land Regions

24   The First People

26   Two Indian Cultures Develop

28   Coastal People

29   Make a Totem Pole

30   Plateau People

31   Learn More on YouTube

32   Exploring Washington

33   Explore the Crossword

34   Exploring by Sea

35   Ocean-in-a-Bottle

36   Exploring by Land

38   Lewis and Clark's Journey

39   The Missionaries

40   Packing for The Oregon Trail

41   The Oregon Trail

42   Field Trip: Naches Pass Trail

43   Trail Maze

44   Two New Territories

45   Write a Treaty

46   The Treaty-Making Era

48   Becoming a State

49   Washington State Fun Facts

50   Levels of Government

52   Our Rights, Our Laws

53   Legal-Eagle Word Search

54   Law Scramble

55   Field Trip: Visit a Government Office

56   Red Light/Green Light

57   Our Responsibilities

58   Make a Fingerprint Flag

59   A Helpful Town

60   The Elements of Our Economy

61   Field Trip: Everyday Economics

62   How It's Made

63   Washington's Industries

64   Field Trip: Apple Orchard

65   Apple Crisp

66   Global Trade

68   My Favorite Things

HOW TO USE A DICTIONARY OR GLOSSARY

When you want to know the meaning of a term in this book, you can look it up in a dictionary or in the book's Glossary (page 256). In both places, terms are listed in alphabetical order, beginning with terms that start with the letter A. Terms are easier to find in the Glossary because there are fewer terms than there are in a dictionary. Try it out!

Find the term GEOGRAPHY in the Glossary. On which page did you find it?

_____

Which terms were listed before and after GEOGRAPHY?

_____

_____

Find the term HISTORY in the Glossary. On which page did you find it?

_____

What does it mean?

_____

_____

_____

_____

What are the first and the last terms listed in the Glossary?

_____

_____

People use many different kinds of dictionaries, including dictionaries printed as books and dictionaries published online. Dictionaries provide a lot of information about a term, such as whether it is a noun, a verb, or another part of speech. Dictionaries also list multiple meanings of a word. Our Glossary only lists the meaning that specifically relates to our study of Washington.

Because they include so many terms, printed dictionaries have guidewords at the top of each page. These words tell you the first and last terms on the page so you know where you are in the alphabet. Online dictionaries do not use guidewords. Use a dictionary to look up the following terms:

Look up the term GEOGRAPHY. What information about the term did you find that was not in the Glossary?

_____

_____

_____

_____

_____

_____

_____

_____

_____

Look up the term HISTORY. What information about the term did you find that was not in the Glossary?

_____

_____

_____

_____

_____

_____

_____

_____

_____

Now you're ready to study the terms that are important to understand as you get to know your state—Washington!

The letters in the hidden message are hidden between the words in this word search. When you find all the words, the hidden message will be revealed.

```
L  E  A  R  N  H  I  N  G  A  B  O  U  H  Y
T  W  A  S  C  H  I  N  G  T  O  N  I  I  H
S  F  U  E  N  V  U  Y  C  S  U  S  E  B  P
E  Q  E  C  W  E  L  K  B  P  T  V  A  L  A
C  P  O  H  L  U  L  Q  M  O  U  L  E  R  R
S  D  G  L  O  S  S  A  R  Y  Y  D  U  V  G
W  G  E  D  R  O  W  Y  N  U  V  I  O  R  O
Y  N  Y  F  B  L  Z  O  T  E  B  C  C  B  E
K  G  T  B  I  T  U  G  R  E  O  T  E  I  G
R  N  D  T  N  N  A  B  N  W  O  I  F  Q  K
S  T  Z  P  P  Y  I  A  C  I  K  O  L  L  Q
Z  T  B  R  S  P  S  T  G  M  N  N  Y  Y  W
T  Z  O  H  A  V  K  Y  I  T  N  A  P  O  U
I  X  U  R  Y  K  P  R  J  O  J  R  E  G  L
I  N  F  O  R  M  A  T  I  O  N  Y  X  M  H
```

BOOK
DEFINITION
DICTIONARY
GEOGRAPHY

GLOSSARY
HISTORY
INFORMATION
MEANING

NOUN
SPEECH
VERB
WORD

__ __ __ __ __ __ __ __ __ __ __

__ __ __ __ __ __ __ __ __ __ __ __ __ __ !

FIELD TRIP: A DAY AT THE MUSEUM

Visiting a museum is a great way to learn about Washington's history. With the help of an adult, plan a field trip to visit a museum near you. This website lists our state's many museums: www.washingtonmuseumassociation.org/museum-directory.

Which museum did you visit?

_____

_____

_____

_____

What was the most interesting thing you saw?

_____

_____

_____

Why was it so interesting to you?

_____

_____

_____

_____

MANY KINDS OF HISTORY

The words below describe ways we can learn more about Washington's history. Use the Glossary (page 256) to find their definitions and complete the chart.

GLOSSARY WORDS	DEFINITIONS
ARTIFACT	
AUTOBIOGRAPHY	
BIOGRAPHY	
HISTORY	
ORAL HISTORY	
PORTRAIT	

MY ARTIFACT

Draw a picture of an artifact that a future historian might discover about you.

TOOLS OF HISTORY

When historians study history, they look for clues about the past. As they search for information, they ask many questions about people, places, and time. Learn more about being a "history detective" by matching each word below with its definition. Time yourself! How long did it take you? _____

WORDS

1. _____ century

2. _____ chronological

3. _____ decade

4. _____ document

5. _____ era

6. _____ historian

7. _____ point of view

8. _____ primary source

9. _____ secondary source

DEFINITIONS

A – information made later, after the event happened

B – a person who studies many sources to learn about events of the past

C – arranged in the order of time

D – an object or writing made by a person who was there at the time

E – the way a person sees an event

F – an official government paper

G – a time period of 100 years

H – a time period of 10 years

I – a period of years when related events happened

FILL IN THE BLANK

Fill in the missing letters for each Glossary word.

1. C_NTURY

2. _HRON_LOGICA_

3. DE_A_E

4. DOC_ME_T

5. _R_

6. HIST_RI_N

7. P_IN_ OF _IE_

8. _RI_A_Y S_URC_

9. S_CO_DA_Y _O_RCE

WHERE IN THE WORLD ARE WE?

Do you know where Washington State fits on a map of the world?

CONTINENT   COUNTRY   STATE   WORLD

1. Our _____ is the planet Earth.

2. Our _____ is North America.

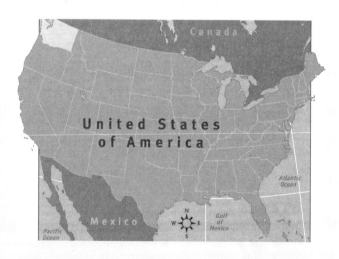

3. Our _____ is the United States of America. What countries are north and south of us?

4. Our _____ is Washington. What states are next to Washington?

_____

_____

_____

_____

Now imagine you're a famous author. Write a summary for the back cover of a book you've written about Washington's place in the world. Give your book a title and color the back cover.

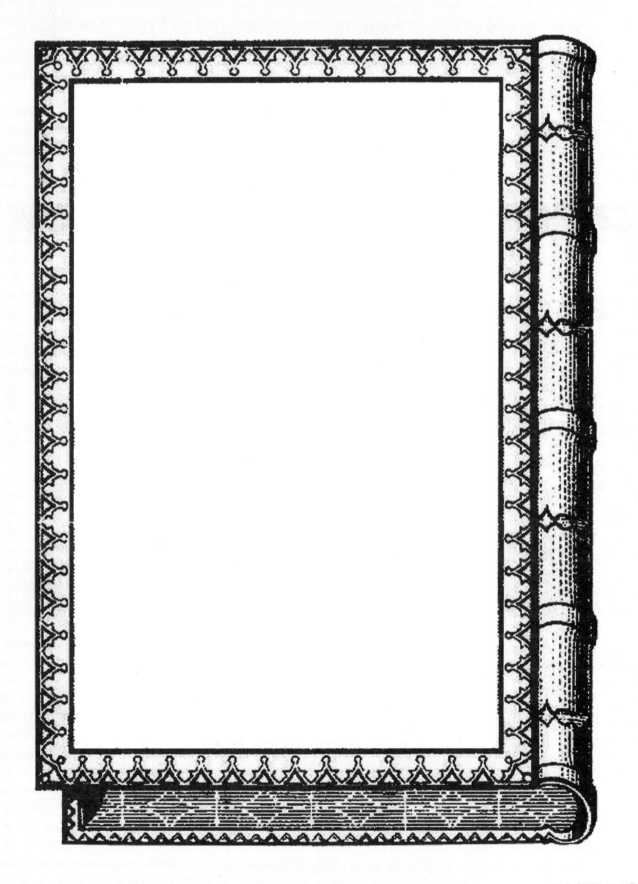

THE LAND WE CALL HOME

Washington State is a beautiful place to call home. From its sandy beaches to its towering mountains, Washington is full of amazing natural features.

Washington State is also full of WATER. Follow each of our state's waterways with a blue crayon or marker. Color in each lake, harbor, and bay. Don't forget to include the Pacific Ocean! Then draw a star on each waterway you've visited.

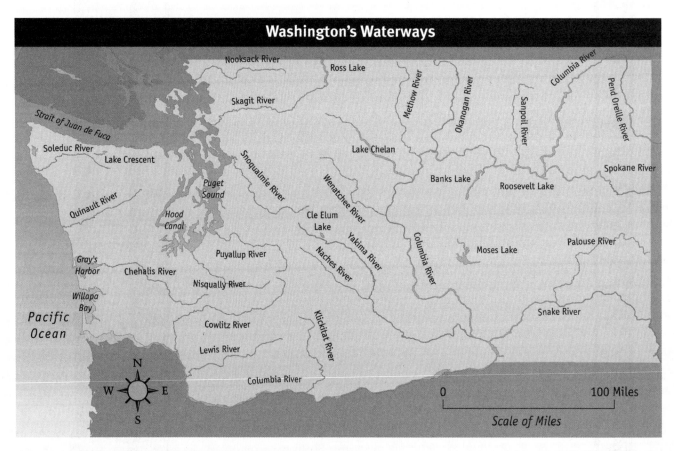

Washington's Waterways

How do you like to have fun in the water?

_____

_____

_____

_____

Let's learn more! Have you ever heard of a KIM chart? KIM stands for **Key** Idea, Additional **Information**, and **Memory** Clue. Complete the KIM chart below using words from the Glossary (page 256). The first example is done for you.

	KEY IDEA	ADDITIONAL INFORMATION	MEMORY CLUE
climate	weather	pattern over years	
cultural characteristics			
elevation			
landform			
natural resource			
physical characteristics			
population			
rural			
urban			

HIKE THE MAZE

The land we call home is a-MAZE-ing! Find your way from Olympia to Spokane.

OLYMPIA

SPOKANE

SNAPSHOTS OF WASHINGTON

Fill each frame with a drawing of something interesting that you've seen in Washington.

LAND REGIONS

Washington State and its neighbor, Oregon, are located in a region called the Pacific Northwest. Washington is divided into five geographical areas called **land regions**. The name of each of Washington's land regions gives you clues about its natural features. Circle the land region where YOU live.

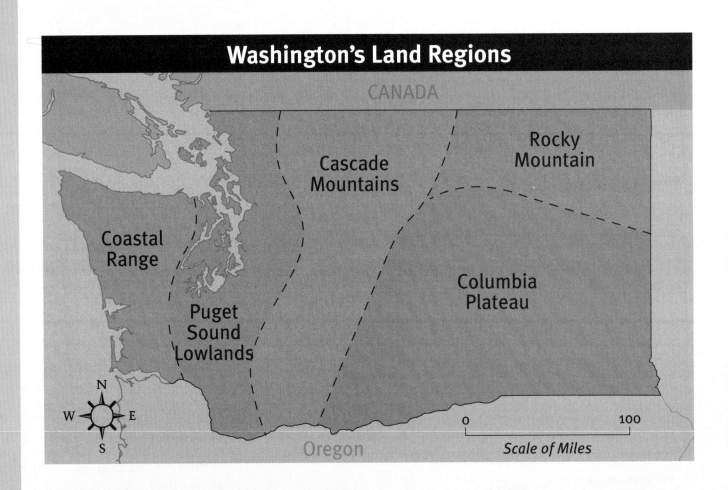

Washington's Land Regions

CANADA

Rocky Mountain

Cascade Mountains

Coastal Range

Columbia Plateau

Puget Sound Lowlands

N
W   E
S

0   100
Scale of Miles

Oregon

Using the Glossary words below, add or change the word ending(s) to make new words. Write each word's new meaning. If the word ending cannot be changed, use the original word in a sentence.

WORD	NEW ENDING(S)	NEW SPELLING	NEW MEANING
1. agriculture	al	_____	_____ _____
2. industry	es	_____	_____ _____
3. irrigation	None of these word endings can be added to irrigation. Use irrigation in a sentence. _____		
4. region	s	_____	_____ _____
5. timber	None of these word endings can be added to timber. Use timber in a sentence. _____		
6. tourism	ist ing	_____ _____	_____ _____

THE FIRST PEOPLE

Scientists refer to Washington's first people as Paleo-Indians. Native Americans call them the Ancient Ones. Ancient means they came to our state long, long ago. Using the clues below, unscramble each Glossary word to learn more about our state's original inhabitants.

ANCIENT   ARCHEOLOGIST   ATLATL   DESCENDANT
EXTINCT   NATIVE   PETROGLYPH

1. TEVIAN
Being a _____ means being born or raised in a certain place or region.

2. GSITHCRAAEOLO
An _____ is a scientist who studies clues to learn how people lived in the past.

3. PHLYGEPTRO
A rock carving is called a _____.

4. INETANC
If something is _____, it is relating to a time long, long ago.

5. ANTSEDDSCNE
_____ refers to people who are children, grandchildren, great-grandchildren, and so on.

6. NCTIXET
If an animal is _____, it is no longer living anywhere on the Earth.

7. LTALTA
An _____ is a tool used to throw a spear farther and faster.

Choose one Glossary word from the preceding page and draw a picture to help you remember what it means.

TWO INDIAN CULTURES DEVELOP

Over time, Washington's Paleo-Indians divided into two groups. The first group, Coastal Indians, lived by the sea. The second group, Plateau Indians, lived far away from the ocean. Notice how the regions where they lived are divided by the Cascade Mountains.

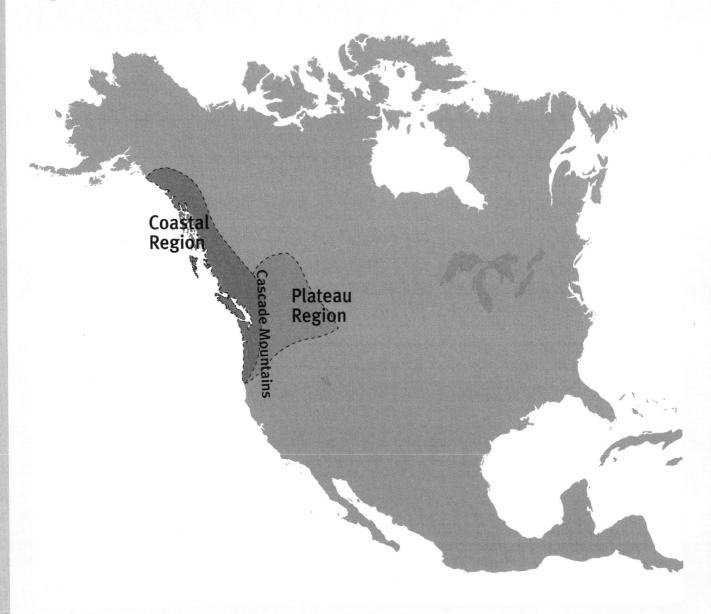

Coastal Region

Cascade Mountains

Plateau Region

WHERE DID THE WORD "INDIAN" COME FROM?

When Christopher Columbus first arrived in America, he thought he was near India. He called the people who lived there Indians. It soon became clear that Columbus had made a mistake, but the name stuck.
Today, we use the words "Indian," "American Indian," and "Native American." Native means born in a place, or being naturally from a place.

Are you a native of Washington State?

_____

If so, where are you from?

_____

If not, where were you born?

_____

Have you lived any other places?

_____

_____

_____

COASTAL PEOPLE

Pretend you are a child in a coastal village. What would you do each day? If you are a boy, you would hunt, fish, and learn to make tools. If you are a girl, you would help gather and prepare food, make clothes, and take care of babies. Throughout your life, the ocean and forests would be very important to you and your family.

Here are some other things that would be important to you. Use the Glossary words below to complete the crossword puzzle.

CEREMONY   HARPOON   LEGEND   POTLATCH   TRADITION   WEIR

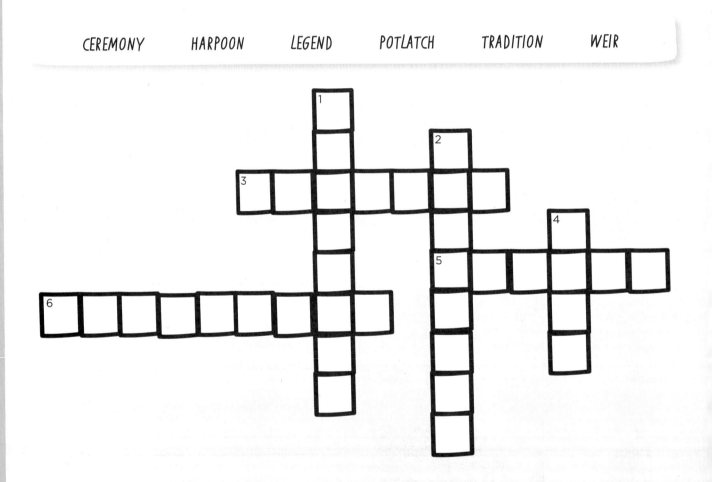

Across
3. a long spear used to hunt whales
5. a story that tells about the past or how things came to be
6. a way of doing something the same way your ancestors did it

Down
1. a ritual; actions done the same way each time for a special purpose
2. a ceremony of feasting and gift-giving
4. a fence built across a stream to catch fish

MAKE A TOTEM POLE

YOU WILL NEED:

Construction paper
Empty paper towel rolls
Tape or glue
Crayons or markers
Scissors

INSTRUCTIONS:

1. Wrap paper around an empty paper towel roll.
2. Decorate it to represent your family.
3. Be creative as you add faces, decorations, and designs.

PLATEAU PEOPLE

Living on the plateau was very different from living near the ocean.
Use the Glossary words below to learn more about plateau culture.

BARTER   BELIEF   ELDER   LONGHOUSE   SHAMAN   SPIRITUAL   TULE

1. _____ having to do with the spirit life and not the physical

2. _____ to trade without using money

3. _____ tall plants that grow wild in swampy places; cattails

4. _____ something thought to be true

5. _____ spiritual leaders who tried to heal the sick

6. _____ long Indian homes where several families lived together

7. _____ an older person

Now use each of these Glossary words in
a sentence.

longhouse

_____

barter

_____

_____   shaman

belief

_____

_____   spiritual

elder

_____

_____   tule

_____

LEARN MORE ON YOUTUBE

A student like you made this video about Washington's Coastal and Plateau Indians for his class at school. Take a look!

Coastal and Plateau Tribes of Washington

www.youtube.com/watch?v=1za5YXjPlok

*Be sure an adult knows you are going online. Only watch YouTube videos that have been approved by your parents or guardians.

What are three things you learned from the video?

_____

_____

_____

EXPLORING WASHINGTON

Native Americans lived in the Pacific Northwest for thousands of years before other people in the world even knew this region existed! Beginning in the 1500s, people from other places finally started to explore our lands. They came here hoping to find treasures, claim land, and trade with the Indians.

Have you ever been on an exploration?

Complete the storyboard by sketching nine steps of an exploration you have taken.

1. What did you explore?

_____

2. Who did you explore with?

_____

3. Why did you explore?

_____

4. What did you learn?

_____

EXPLORE THE CROSSWORD

To explore means to travel to a new place to learn more about it. Here are some other terms about exploration. Complete the crossword puzzle with words from our Glossary.

CLAIM   ENCOUNTER   EXPLORE   FUR TRADE   PELT   TRADE ROUTE

Across
3. meeting face to face
5. to take as a rightful owner
6. a business where animal fur is traded for other things or for money

Down
1. a route over water or land that is used by traders
2. the skin of an animal with the fur still attached
4. to travel to a new place to learn about it

EXPLORING BY SEA

Washington's first explorers came from three countries. Unscramble the names of each country. Copy the letters in the numbered boxes to find the missing word in the sentence below.

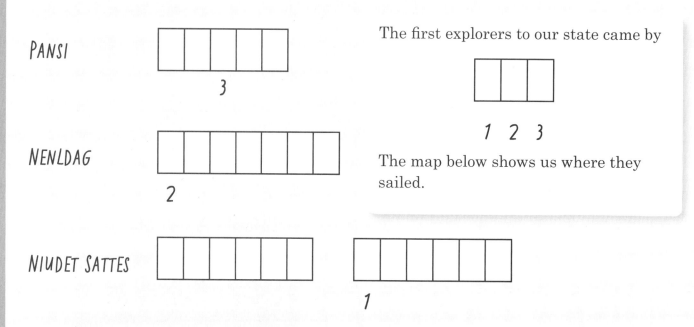

PANSI

[ ][ ][ ][ ][ ]
3

NENLDAG

[ ][ ][ ][ ][ ][ ][ ]
2

NIUDET SATTES

[ ][ ][ ][ ][ ][ ]   [ ][ ][ ][ ][ ][ ]
1

The first explorers to our state came by

[ ][ ][ ]
1 2 3

The map below shows us where they sailed.

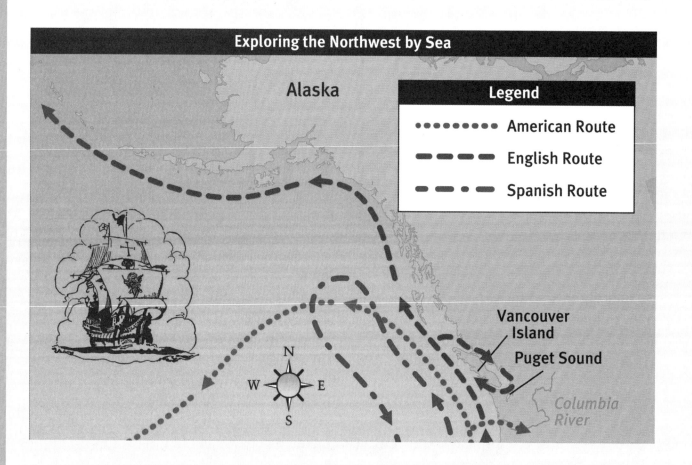

Exploring the Northwest by Sea

Alaska

Legend

•••••••• American Route

– – – – English Route

– – · – Spanish Route

Vancouver Island

Puget Sound

Columbia River

N W E S

OCEAN-IN-A-BOTTLE

See the SEA at home with this fun craft.

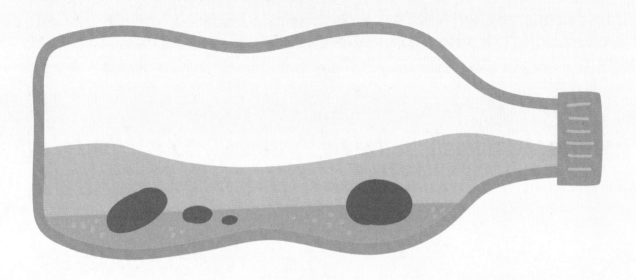

YOU WILL NEED:

$^1/_4$ cup sand
10 small seashells
1 clear plastic beverage container
Green and blue food coloring
Water
Silver glitter
Mineral or baby oil
Hot glue gun

DIRECTIONS:

1. Pour sand and shells into the clean bottle.
2. Mix a drop each of blue and green food coloring into 6 cups of water then fill the bottle halfway. Discard remaining water.
3. Add a pinch of glitter.
4. Fill the rest of the bottle with oil, leaving ½ inch of airspace at the top.
5. With the help of a grown-up, run a bead of hot glue around the bottle opening and screw the lid on quickly.

EXPLORING BY LAND

After the first brave sailors explored Washington's coastlines, explorers from Canada and the United States explored our lands. Fill in each blank with words from the Glossary to learn more about their difficult journeys. Then find each of these words in the word search.

| EXPEDITION | INTERPRETER | OVERLAND | RAPIDS | SLAVE | TERRAIN |

1. After explorers came by ship, more explorers came _____.

2. A _____ is a person who is owned by another person.

3. Lewis and Clark led an _____ to the Northwest region.

4. An _____ helped the explorers speak with the Indians.

5. Often, the _____ explorers had to cross was unknown and dangerous

6. _____ can make traveling on a river very dangerous.

```
N  I  A  R  R  E  T  D  O  V  E  R  A  N  D
O  E  P  N  N  O  S  D  N  A  L  R  E  V  O
S  S  R  N  E  A  T  T  I  D  E  P  X  E  V
L  S  E  X  E  D  I  T  I  O  N  I  P  D  I
A  D  P  I  N  T  E  R  P  R  E  T  E  R  R
V  I  I  E  L  V  D  T  E  R  R  A  I  T  I
I  P  D  I  A  P  S  L  N  T  L  R  E  V  O
R  A  S  L  A  I  N  T  E  R  P  E  T  E  R
I  R  S  R  E  X  P  E  D  I  T  I  O  N  D
V  E  E  R  D  S  I  P  P  X  A  V  R  N  S
```

LEWIS AND CLARK'S JOURNEY

The most famous explorers to reach Washington by land were Meriwether Lewis and William Clark. Use a blue crayon to trace their journey by river. Use a **red** crayon to trace their journey by horse. Use your favorite color to circle each Indian group.

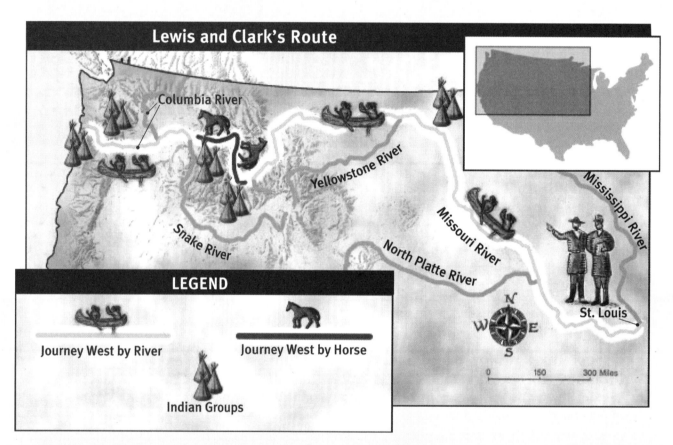

Lewis and Clark's Route

Columbia River

Yellowstone River

Snake River

Missouri River

North Platte River

Mississippi River

St. Louis

LEGEND

Journey West by River

Journey West by Horse

Indian Groups

0   150   300 Miles

Learn More Online:
Visit www.nationalgeographic.com/west/main.html to go on an interactive expedition of your own. (This Lewis & Clark game was developed by *National Geographic Kids*. Make sure an adult knows whenever you use the Internet.)

THE MISSIONARIES

As fur traders and pioneers began to settle our state, they wanted to share their religion with the Indians. Churches started sending missionaries to teach the Indians about their beliefs. Would you like to learn more about missionaries in Washington? Use the Glossary terms in the word bank to complete the passage below.

DISEASE   MASSACRE   MISSIONARIES   ORPHANAGE
RELIGION   TRAGEDY   CONVERT

In 1834, the first_____came to the Northwest. They were

people who came to teach their way of life and _____to Indians.

They wanted to _____Indians to a new way of thinking about

religion.

Missions were a nice place for travelers to stop as they passed through.

However, travelers brought _____s that killed many Indians.

This made the Indians angry. One day, a group of Cayuse attacked the Whitman

mission. This event was a _____. Thirteen people were killed.

Fur traders and trappers started calling the murder a _____

because a large group of people was killed. The Indians thought that they needed to

kill the missionaries to save their people from disease.

After the tragedy, some missionaries left the Northwest and others stayed.

About 10 years after the Whitmans, Mother Joseph came to the area. She

started many small hospitals and schools for Indian children. She also opened an

_____ for children who had no parents to care for them.

PACKING FOR THE OREGON TRAIL

Before there were roads leading to the Pacific Northwest, travelers had to make their own trails. What became known as the **Oregon Trail** is the route people took to Washington.

Some people came to our state for adventure. Some came to avoid slavery. Most came for the promise of land.

Imagine that it is 1850 and your family has decided to leave the busy Northeast to move to the Northwest, where they can get free land. Complete the packing list below to help you decide what you will be able to take with you.

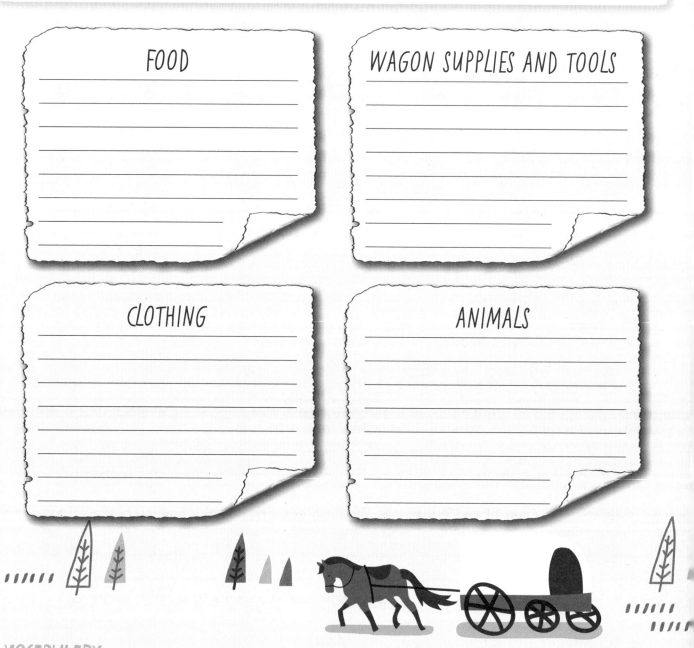

FOOD

WAGON SUPPLIES AND TOOLS

CLOTHING

ANIMALS

THE OREGON TRAIL

Fill in the blanks with words from the Glossary to learn more about the Oregon Trail.

BENEFIT   COST   FRONTIER   HARDSHIP
HOMESTEAD   IMMIGRANT   PIONEER   SLAVERY

1. _____ is when people are bought and sold and forced to work for their owners without pay.

2. A _____ is what you get in return for paying the cost.

3. If a person were to _____ , they were to claim, farm, and improve land.

4. A person who moves into a country is an _____ .

5. A _____ is what you give up to get what you want.

6. If someone has a _____ , they are suffering.

7. A region on the edge of settled land is called a _____ .

8. A _____ is a person who is among the first settlers to move to a new place.

FIELD TRIP: NACHES PASS TRAIL

The Naches Pass Trail is considered an extension of the Oregon Trail that branches off the main trail near Walla Walla and ends in Steilacoom. You can view a map of this historic Native American route at http://www.nachestrail.org/media/images/naches_pass_trail_color_map_lg.jpg. You can find a lot more information about the trail at www.nachestrail.org. Remember to let an adult know before you go online!

Today, the Naches Pass Trail is a popular spot for four-wheeling and riding motorcycles. There's also a hiking trail. You can plan a visit with your family by researching online.

If a field trip isn't possible, take a virtual trip by watching this Washington ATV Adventure video: www.youtube.com/watch?v=m2mpwB2ZHAc.

What do you think it would have been like to travel on this trail by wagon?

_____

_____

_____

_____

Write one adjective between each spoke of this wagon wheel to describe your journey.

TRAIL MAZE

Help the immigrants find Washington by drawing a path for them to follow in the maze.

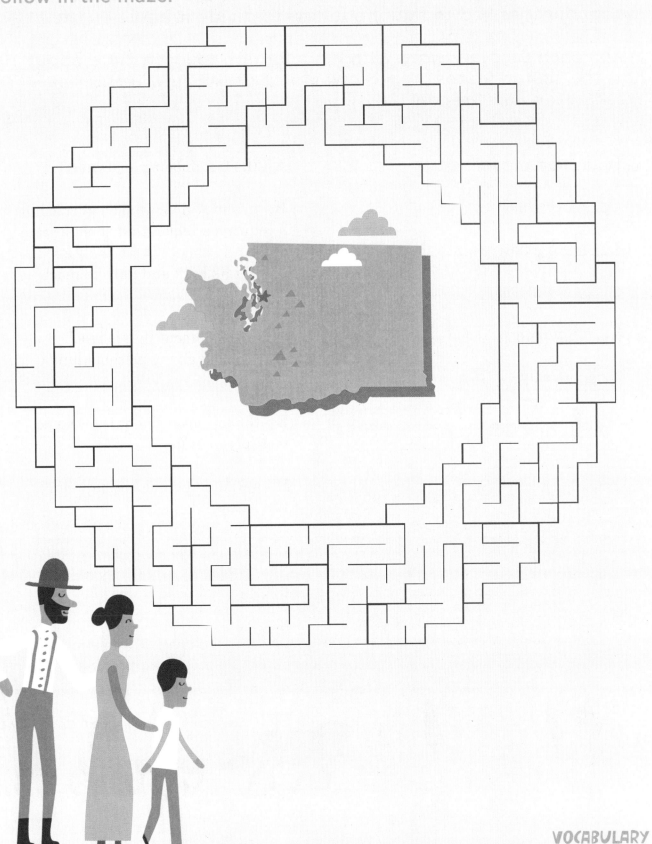

TWO NEW TERRITORIES

As settlers continued to arrive in the Pacific Northwest, Britain and the United States both claimed ownership of the land. Leaders of these countries had to figure out how to divide it between them.

Match each Glossary word with its definition to learn more about how the United States gained ownership of two new territories—Washington and Oregon.

1. _____ compromise

2. _____ governor

3. _____ negotiate

4. _____ ownership

5. _____ territory

6. _____ treaty

A – the fact of being an owner

B – a land region owned and ruled by a country; a region that is not a state

C – to talk back and forth to reach an agreement

D – an agreement that is reached by each side giving up something it wants

E – the top government leader of a territory or state

F – a written agreement between two groups

WRITE A TREATY

Using the words COMPROMISE, NEGOTIATE, OWNERSHIP, and TERRITORY, write a treaty about dividing space in your bedroom that you share with your brother or sister.

COMPROMISE   NEGOTIATE   OWNERSHIP   TERRITORY

_____

_____

_____

_____

_____

_____

_____

_____

_____

THE TREATY-MAKING ERA

After Washington Territory was created, the U.S. government made treaties with the Indians. It was a time of change for the Indians, and treaties were negotiated to try to solve problems.

Complete this puzzle about the treaty-making era by matching the correct Glossary word to its definition.

CONFLICT   COUNCIL   DEFEND   FERTILE   LUMBER
PERSPECTIVE   PROFITABLE   RESERVATION   SURRENDER

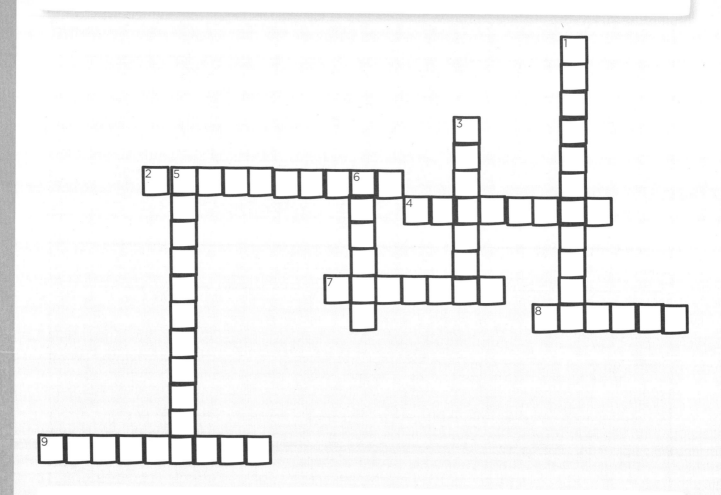

Across
2. able to make money
4. problem between two people or groups
7. good for growing crops
8. to drive away danger or attack
9. to give up

Down
1. point of view
3. a meeting where a group of people make decisions
5. land set aside for Native Americans
6. logs sawed into boards

A treaty is like a promise.

Look up these words in a dictionary and write the meanings.

promise:

_____

contract:

_____

treaty:

_____

Look at the cartoons. These people are making promises to each other. Write what you think each person is saying.

BECOMING A STATE

Extra, extra! Read all about it! In 1889, Washington became the United States' 42nd state! Mining in the Pacific Northwest, expansion of the railroad, and population growth made Washington's statehood possible. Write and illustrate a news article sharing this exciting news.

Include these words from the Glossary (page 256): **COMMUNITY**, **GOLD RUSH**, and **OPPORTUNITY**.

Washington Times
November 11, 1889

HEADLINE: _____

WASHINGTON STATE FUN FACTS

Visit **www.del. wa.gov/kids/ wafunfacts.aspx** to learn some fun facts about our state! *Remember to let an adult know whenever you go online.

Do you know something unique about Washington that wasn't on the list? Write it here.

_____

_____

_____

_____

_____

_____

Now, email YOUR fun fact to **communications@del.wa.gov**. Maybe they'll post it on their website!

LEVELS OF GOVERNMENT

Washington State's government was created to provide order and protect the people. Use the definitions below to help you unscramble these Glossary words about government.

CONSTITUTION   COUNTY   ENFORCE   REPRESENTATIVE
SOVEREIGNTY   TAX   TRIBAL COUNCIL

1. *NTYVOSEREIG* _____

self-rule; supreme power or authority

2. *XTA* _____

money people must pay to the government

3. *NIOTCONTUSTI* _____

a written plan for government

4. *SENTPRERETIVETA* _____

a person elected to vote for other people

5. *TYNOUC* _____

a government region within a state

6. *BLARIT NCCOUIL* _____ _____

a group that makes laws for an Indian tribe on Indian lands

7. *NFOECER* _____

to make sure people obey (a law or rule)

Every person who lives in Washington State lives under several levels of government.

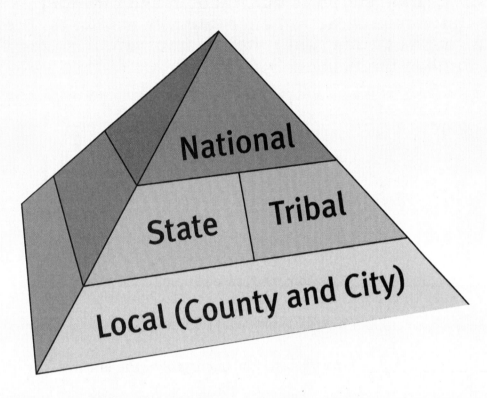

Local governments make laws and rules for people in towns, cities, and counties.

State governments make laws for the people in each state.

Tribal governments make laws for American Indians on tribal lands.

Our **national government** makes laws for everyone in the United States.

What is the name of your county?

_____

What is the name of your city or town?

_____

Do you live on tribal lands? If so, which tribe?

_____

OUR RIGHTS, OUR LAWS

Washington's constitution supports our freedom and our rights. The laws of our state are created to help protect these rights. The sentences below teach us about our rights and our laws. Use the Glossary words to fill in the blanks.

BILL	RIGHTS	IDEAL	RULE OF LAW	LIBERTY	VETO

1._____ the privileges citizens are entitled to

2. _____ freedom; the state of being free

3._____ a written proposal for a law

4._____ the idea that no one is above the law; the law is the highest power

5._____ an idea about the way things should be; something that is believed to be perfect or best

6._____ to say no to a bill; to prevent a bill from becoming a law

LEGAL-EAGLE WORD SEARCH

Use the glossary words from the previous page as hint to find the hidden words. Circle the words when you find them.

```
Y S B B E L S T H G I R F I T
T E T A E A H I R L D R W R H
R F D E G E A E R I G H T E I
E I B L B D L I B E T Y B V
B T R I L I O S L D T B I I
I I L U L F O E L U R L O L U
L R U L E U F L A W S R I V F
R I R U L E O F L A W W U B V
E L A D B L D O T E V E L L B
R A L V L I I E I L A L E H F
```

LAW SCRAMBLE

In our country, there is no king. Instead, we follow the rule of the law. Unscramble the tiles to reveal a message about the importance of having laws.

MUS	EY T	THAT	AIR	YONE	HING
OW T	AY F	HE L	AW	EVER	T OB
S ST	'S H				

FIELD TRIP: VISIT A GOVERNMENT OFFICE

See Washington State government in action! Take a field trip to see government working for YOU! With the help of an adult, make arrangements to visit a nearby office of government. You can find information about government offices online, in phone books, and at your local library. Take plenty of notes.

Examples of places to visit: City buildings, police stations, county offices, the State Capitol, federal buildings, post offices, etc.

Which government office did you visit?

_____

What did you do there?

_____

_____

What did you learn about on your visit?

_____

_____

_____

_____

_____

RED LIGHT/GREEN LIGHT

Imagine what might happen if Washington State had no traffic laws to help drivers stay safe on our streets. Driving safely is serious business!

Here's a fun game to help you and your friends remember some rules of the road.

In this game, one person pretends to be the "stoplight," and the rest of the players race to touch him or her without getting caught in motion.

At the beginning of the game, all of the players form a line about 30 feet away from the stoplight.

The stoplight faces away from the other players and calls, "Green light!" At this point, the players move quickly toward the stoplight.

At any point in the game, the stoplight may suddenly call, "Red light!" and turn around to face the other players. All of the players must freeze in place. If any of the players are caught moving, they are out of the game.

Play resumes when the stoplight turns back around and says, "Green light." The stoplight wins if all the players are out before anyone is able to touch him/her. Otherwise, the first player to touch the stoplight wins and earns the right to be the "stoplight" for the next round of the game.

OUR RESPONSIBILITIES

We all have special jobs to do to make Washington a wonderful place to live. These responsibilities include obeying the laws, taking care of our homes and families, and getting involved in our communities. Adults also have a responsibility to vote in local, state, and national elections.

Each term below is related to our responsibilities as citizens. Use the Glossary (page 256) or a dictionary to help you write a definition for each of these important words. Then use each term in a sentence.

1. CITIZEN - Definition: _____

Sentence: _____

2. CIVIC - Definition: _____

Sentence: _____

3. DUTY - Definition: _____

Sentence: _____

4. ELECTION - Definition: _____

Sentence: _____

5. POLITICS - Definition: _____

Sentence: _____

6. RESPONSIBILITY - Definition: _____

Sentence: _____

7. VOLUNTEER - Definition: _____

Sentence: _____

MAKE A FINGERPRINT FLAG

Someday, you might leave a personal mark on local, state, tribal, or national government! Even if you don't become a political leader, everyone in Washington State has the opportunity to serve our communities in some way.

Make a fingerprint flag of the United States in the below space.

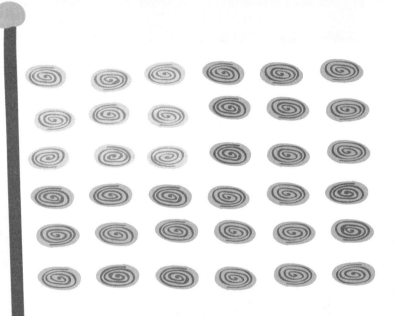

YOU WILL NEED:

a blue stamp pad
a red stamp pad

DIRECTIONS:

1. Make the flag's "stars" with blue fingerprints.
2. Make the flag's "stripes" with red fingerprints.
3. Think about the "fingerprint" you might leave on society someday.

A HELPFUL TOWN

Study the drawing of the town to find ways that people, places, and things help the citizens of this town.

Ways that people in this town are helping each other:

_____

_____

_____

Ways that things and places in this town help the citizens:

_____

_____

_____

_____

THE ELEMENTS OF OUR ECONOMY

Washington's economy is like a puzzle, with pieces related to geography, natural resources, climate, and labor. Use the Glossary words to complete a crossword puzzle about this important topic.

CONSERVE   ECONOMICS   GOODS   HYDROELECTRICITY
   LABOR   RESERVOIR   SERVICES   SUSTAIN

Across
3. the study of how people produce, sell, and buy goods and services
4. things that are made and then bought and sold
5. electricity produced by water power
7. a large lake used as a source of water
8. to support or strengthen

Down
1. workers; working
2. to protect or save something for the future
6. in economics, work people do for other people for money

FIELD TRIP: EVERYDAY ECONOMICS

You can learn more about Washington's economy by visiting a place of business. Take a field trip with your family to a bank, store, or factory.

Where did you go?

_____

Why did you choose to go to this business?

_____

What did you see?

_____

What kind of services did this business provide to you?

_____

Does the business make any goods?

_____

How many people work there?

_____

What did you learn?

_____

HOW IT'S MADE

Industry refers to the manufacture of goods and services in an economy. Have you ever wondered how a product is made?

Visit **www.neok12.com/ Industry.htm** to watch videos for kids about how toothbrushes, plastic bags, bicycles, and other products are manufactured. Remember to let an adult know whenever you go online!

Choose four videos to watch.

Which videos did you watch?

_____

_____

_____

_____

What did you find most interesting?

_____

_____

_____

_____

Why?

_____

_____

_____

_____

WASHINGTON'S INDUSTRIES

Look up the words below in the Glossary (page 256). Complete the chart by writing two or three key words from each definition. Then make a sketch to help you remember what each word means.

	KEY WORDS	SKETCH
consumer		
distributor		
livestock		
processed		
producer		
product		
technology		

FIELD TRIP: APPLE ORCHARD

Did you know that about 70 percent of the apples sold in the United States are produced in Washington? Apples are a very important part of our state's economy! Here's a video you can watch to learn more: www.youtube.com/watch?v=FmCRchd5k08.

Visiting an apple orchard is another great way to learn more about Washington's apple industry. With the help of an adult, do some online research to find an orchard near you!

PLAN YOUR APPLE-PICKING TRIP:

Where are you going to go?

_____

What will you take with you?

_____

What type(s) of apples does this orchard produce?

_____

AFTER YOUR VISIT:

Do you think you'd like to work in the apple industry? Why or why not?

_____

_____

APPLE CRISP

Now that you have visited an apple orchard and know all about the apple industry, let's do something tasty!

With the help of an adult, make this recipe for Apple Crisp at your house.

Apple Crisp

INGREDIENTS

3 pounds (about 8–10) tart apples, cored and thinly sliced

1 tablespoon lemon juice

$^2/_3$ cup granulated Splenda

2 teaspoons cinnamon

$^1/_4$ teaspoon nutmeg

$^1/_4$ teaspoons ginger

8 square graham crackers

4 ginger snap cookies

$^1/_2$ cup ground nuts

$^1/_2$ cup (1 stick) butter or margarine, melted

DIRECTIONS

Preheat oven to 350 degrees. Prepare an 8 x 10-inch baking dish with nonstick cooking spray.

Cut apple slices in half and arrange in baking dish. Sprinkle lemon juice over apples.

In a medium bowl, mix together the Splenda, cinnamon, nutmeg, and ginger. Sprinkle evenly over apples.

In a food processor, process crackers and cookies to a fine crumb. Transfer crumbs to a bowl and stir in nuts. Pour a third of the butter over crumb mixture and mix to moisten. Pour another third of the butter into the crumbs and mix well. If crumbs are sufficiently moistened (they don't have to stick together), drizzle remaining butter over the apples.

Distribute crumbs loosely over the apples. Bake for 45–50 minutes, until apples are cooked and crumbs begin to brown. Makes 8–10 servings.

GLOBAL TRADE

Trade has always been an important part of Washington's economy. We trade with partners all around the world.

Want to know more? Use the Glossary (page 256) to help you match each term to the correct meaning.

1. _____ cargo

2. _____ export

3. _____ gateway

4. _____ global

5. _____ import

A – an opening; a way to enter a place

B – to bring goods or services into a country from another country

C – relating to the whole world

D – to ship goods or services out to other countries

E – goods carried on a ship, train, truck, or plane

Now use each of these words in a sentence.

CARGO

_____

_____

EXPORT

_____

_____

GATEWAY

_____

_____

GLOBAL

_____

_____

IMPORT

_____

_____

MY FAVORITE THINGS

Brainstorm a list of your favorite products or things that you use and play with.

After brainstorming, choose one of the products to research. Fill out the information about your product and include a picture.

MY FAVORITE THINGS

_____   _____

_____   _____

_____   _____

_____   _____

_____   _____

_____   _____

_____   _____

_____   _____

_____   _____

_____   _____

PRODUCT TO RESEARCH:

_____

1. How my product was made:

_____

_____

_____

3. Where my product was made:

_____

_____

_____

2. Materials used to make my product:

_____

_____

_____

4. When my product was made:

_____

_____

_____

Draw or glue a picture of your product below.

GEOGRAPHY & SOCIAL STUDIES

72   Reading and Creating a Timeline

74   State Biography

76   My Place in the World

77   Neighborhood Walk

78   Hemispheres

79   Color the Sphere

80   My Home Geography

81   Make a Mobile!

82   Build a Compass

83   Map Terms Word Search

84   Design a License Plate

86   A Map by Any Other Name . . . Would Still Be a Map

88   Create a Chalk Map of Your Home

89   Field Trip: See a Big City

90   Population Map of Washington

92   Important Places in Washington

93   Land Features Crossword

94   Land Features

96   Relief Map

98   Picturing Washington's Land Regions

101   Field Trip: Coast to the Coast

102   Industry Map

104   National Parks

106   Field Trip: National Park

107   Tourism in Washington

108   This Is Only a Drill

110   Put Yourself in the Picture

112   Paleo-Indians

113   Archaic Indians

114   Archaic and Paleo-Indians

115   Make Your Own Rock Art

116   Indian Tribal Lands

117   Natural Dyes

118   Preserving Meat

119   Lewis and Clark's Journey

120   Lewis and Clark Timeline

122   Fact or Fiction?

123   Comparing Maps

124   The Pig War

125   Act It Out!

126   Find the Hidden Term

127   Favorite State Symbols

READING AND CREATING A TIMELINE

Timelines show us important events that happened during a specific time period. We read timelines from left to right. The event that happened first is recorded on the left. The most recent event is recorded on the right.

Here is an example of a timeline created by a ten-year-old boy named Marcus, who recorded the most important events in his life. Study his timeline and answer the questions below.

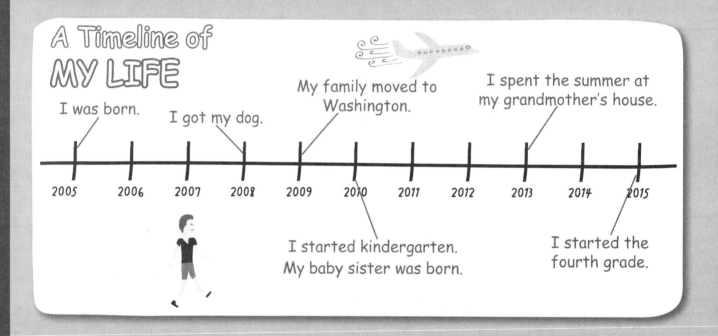

A Timeline of **MY LIFE**

I was born. — I got my dog. — My family moved to Washington. — I spent the summer at my grandmother's house.

2005 2006 2007 2008 2009 2010 2011 2012 2013 2014 2015

I started kindergarten. My baby sister was born. — I started the fourth grade.

1. When was Marcus's baby sister born? How old was Marcus when she was born?

_____

2. What else happened to Marcus the year his sister was born?

_____

3. How many years does the timeline show? Why do you think that is?

_____

_____

Now it's your turn! Create a timeline of your life. Begin with the year you were born and end with the current year. Add evenly spaced marks to the timeline to represent each year of your life. Choose at least 10 important events from your life. Record them on the timeline in the order they happened. You can also include pictures on your timeline. Be creative!

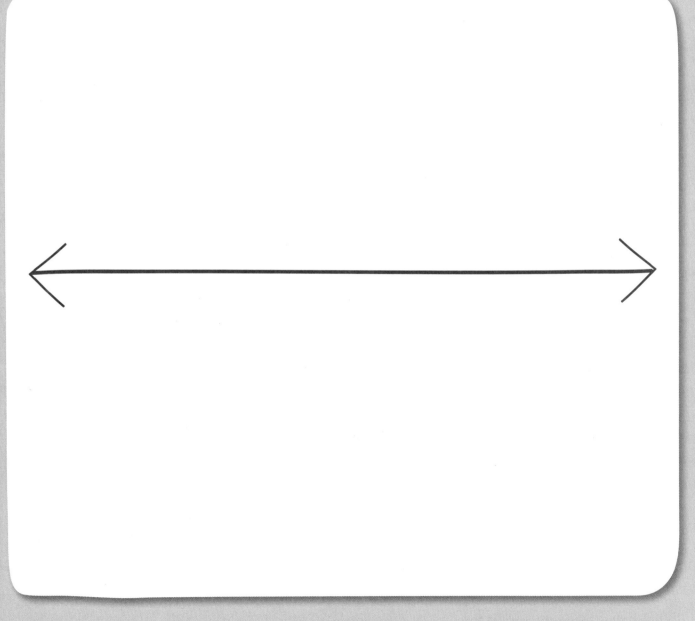

STATE BIOGRAPHY

Many important people have helped shape the history of our state. There are also many people working hard today to make a positive difference in Washington. Choose one of these influential people to study. Choose a person whose life is of high interest to you. Also, make sure you can easily find information about this person, either in books or on the Internet.

See the next page for names of just a few important and interesting people from Washington's history. As you learn more about the person you've chosen, record important details on the character outline provided.

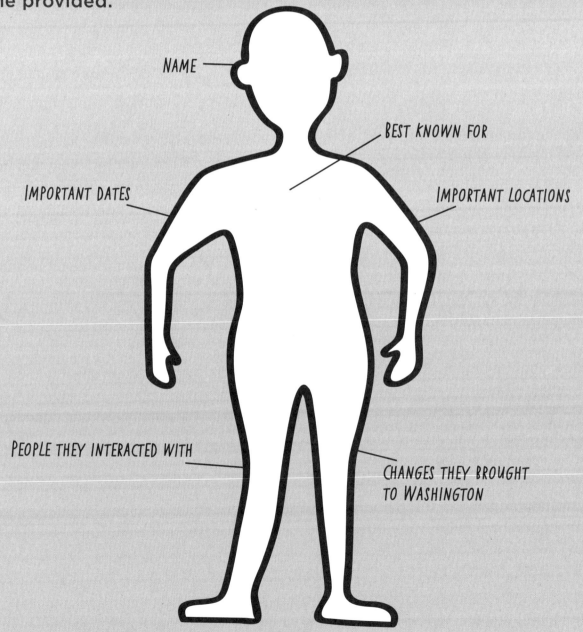

NAME

BEST KNOWN FOR

IMPORTANT DATES

IMPORTANT LOCATIONS

PEOPLE THEY INTERACTED WITH

CHANGES THEY BROUGHT TO WASHINGTON

WILLIAM BOEING	Founded the Boeing Company, whose innovations have positively affected commercial air travel.
JEFFREY BROTMAN	Co-founder of Costco.
DALE CHIHULY	A famous visual artist.
JAMES HILL	Founder of the Great Northern Railway.
RUFUS WOODS	Longtime owner of *Wenatchee Daily Word* and pioneer in bringing hydroelectric power to central Washington.
GORDON HIRABAYASHI	Japanese civil rights activist who was imprisoned during World War II and not released until the 1980s.
FLOYD SCHMOE	A lifelong peace activist who helped refugees and survivors during both World War I and World War II.
GEORGE VANCOUVER	Famous explorer of the Pacific Northwest.
CHIEF JOSEPH	Was a leader of the Nez Perce Tribe who lead a resistance against the U.S. government in 1877.
CHIEF SEATTLE	Was a leader of the Duwamish and Suquamish Tribes in the 1850s.
NARCISSA WHITMAN	She and her husband built a mission in the 1800s and were attacked and killed by Indians.
BILL GATES	Founded Microsoft.

MY PLACE IN THE WORLD

Before we can understand our state, we need to understand where our state fits in and where we fit in! Complete the diagram below starting with yourself to help you understand exactly where you are in the world!

I am a part of a family,

Which is part of

_____
(neighborhood)

Which is part of

_____
(city/town)

Which is part of

_____
(county)

Which is part of

_____
(state)

Which is part of the

_____
(region)

Which is part of

_____
(country)

Which is part of

_____
(continent)

Which is part of

_____
(hemisphere)

Which is part of the planet Earth!

GEOGRAPHY & SOCIAL STUDIES

NEIGHBORHOOD WALK

Take a walk around your neighborhood, the exact same path, at three different times on the same day—in the morning, at midday, and in the evening. What do you observe? Make a list for each walk noting what you see. People, animals, plants, cars, weather, bugs—who knows what else there may be?!

1. MORNING
_____

2. MIDDAY
_____

3. EVENING
_____

Did everything look the same all day long? Or did you observe something different depending on the time of day? Write your observations below.

_____

_____

_____

What day of the week was it when you went on your walk? Do you think you might see something different on other days?

_____

_____

_____

HEMISPHERES

N

W   E

S

To help us understand where things are located, we pretend the Earth is cut into two equal pieces. Each half is called a hemisphere.

**Hemi means half. Sphere means a round, solid shape
Put them together: Half of a round, solid shape**

The equator divides the Earth into hemispheres. The area north of the equator to the north pole is the northern hemisphere. The area south of the equator to the south pole is the southern hemisphere. Because Washington is north of the equator, it is in the northern hemisphere.

The prime meridian splits the Earth in half a different way. The area west of the prime meridian is the western hemisphere. The area east of the prime meridian is the eastern hemisphere. Washington is in the western hemisphere.

Use the compass to help you determine which hemisphere is which. Label each hemisphere.

NORTHERN HEMISPHERE   SOUTHERN HEMISPHERE   WESTERN HEMISPHERE

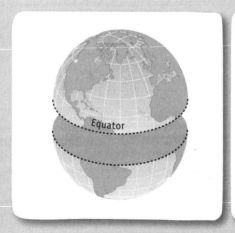

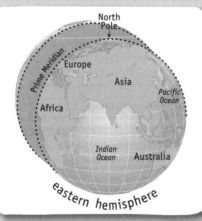

COLOR THE SPHERE

Do you know the names of the imaginary lines we draw to create hemispheres? A line called the equator divides the Earth into its northern and southern hemispheres.

Trace over the equator with a **blue** marker. The area north of the equator to the north pole is called the northern hemisphere. Color it **yellow**. The area south of the equator to the south pole is called the southern hemisphere. Color it **green**.

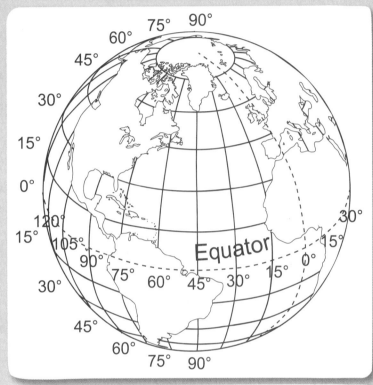

The prime meridian is what we call the line that divides the Earth from east to west. Trace over the prime meridian with a **red** marker. The area west of the prime meridian is called the western hemisphere. Color it **purple**. The area east of the prime meridian is called the eastern hemisphere. Color it **orange**.

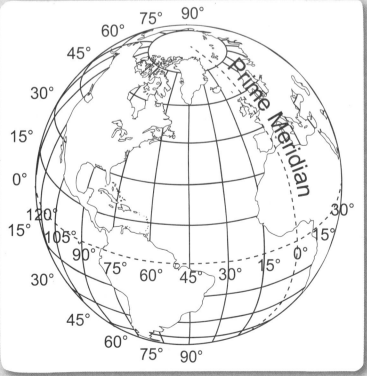

MY HOME GEOGRAPHY

Geography is the study of the land, water, plants, animals, and people of a place. What is the geography like where you live? Use this chart to help you study and learn more about the geography where you live! Share your findings with a family member.

What **landforms** do you see around your house? (mountains, valleys, plateaus, foothills, wetlands, harbors, peninsulas, inlets, capes, islands, straits, etc.)

What sources of **water** are near your home? (lakes, rivers, streams , the ocean, etc.)

What kinds of **plant life** are common where you live?

What kinds of **animals** live near you?

Describe the **people** near where you live. (age, family makeup, religion, culture, jobs, etc.)

MAKE A MOBILE!

Using the information you've gathered about your home's geography, make a mobile to hang in your bedroom. Every time you look at it, you'll be reminded of the interesting geography where you live.

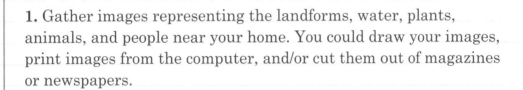

YOU WILL NEED:

Images representing your home's
   geography
Scissors
Crayons or markers
Hole punch
Paint
An empty paper towel roll
Yarn or string
Tape

DIRECTIONS:

1. Gather images representing the landforms, water, plants, animals, and people near your home. You could draw your images, print images from the computer, and/or cut them out of magazines or newspapers.

2. Color and cut out your images. Artistically label the back of each image with its name. Punch a hole in the top of each image.

3. Paint your paper towel roll as desired.

4. Using varied lengths of yarn, tie one end of each strand to an image. Reinforce it with tape. Wrap the other end around your paper towel roll. Tape it in place.

5. Thread a longer piece of yarn through the center of the roll and tie the ends together. This is how you'll hang your mobile.

6. Share your mobile with a family member or friend. Isn't your home's geography amazing?

BUILD A COMPASS

Over 1,000 years ago, the Chinese discovered that a swinging magnet always pointed north. This swinging magnet became the first compass. During the 1400s, Europeans improved the compass. Sailors, who were miles away from shore, used it to figure out direction. Today, many people use a GPS to find directions and locate places. You can make a compass at home!

YOU WILL NEED:

A plastic lid or shallow bowl
A needle or straight pin
A bar magnet
A slice of cork, Styrofoam, or
    the top of a plastic milk jug
Some water

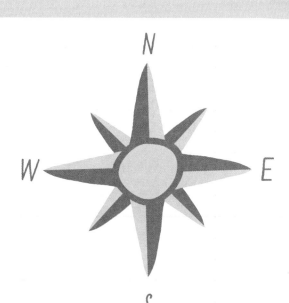

INSTRUCTIONS:

1. Have an adult help you slice off a piece of cork.
2. Magnetize your needle! Hold the needle in one hand and the bar magnet in the other.
3. Taking care to only move in one direction, not back and forth, slide one end of the bar magnet along the length of the needle. Lift up the magnet and slide in the same direction again. Repeat this at least 50 times.
4. Pour some water in the plastic lid.
5. Place the cork in the water and make sure there is enough water for the cork to float.
6. Lay the needle on top of the cork. Make sure the needle is balanced well.
7. The needle will move until it points north. This may take a moment.
8. If your needle isn't pointing north, repeat step two.

CONGRATULATIONS! YOU HAVE MADE A COMPASS!

MAP TERMS WORD SEARCH

It is important to be familiar with terms associated with maps. The terms help you understand the information the maps are providing. Using the terms in the word box, circle the hidden words in the puzzle.

COMPASS ROSE   EAST   EQUATOR   HEMISPHERE   LEGEND   NORTH
PRIME MERIDIAN   SCALE OF MILES   SOUTH   WEST

```
J Z Q U P B D S C A L E O F M I L E S H
P U N W S R B E P H E Q Z J N D Z V E B
L E G E N D I D O O P K N B I Q M M C M
Q K V F E Y Y M W N L I K Z X S I F X J
T W T O H M N M E U D J W F N S M C Z X
E Q U A T O R H C M H L R Z P M N X G X
K H A F L K Q X X L E N Q H T W G M G K
W F U B K I G M X U K R E T T F R O E O
E Q J Z Z F V G R D J R I V M S D E J M
U U C O R R V H Z T E Y I D B G A R S J
Z U A V R H X E E T S O O G I V T E U H
O D C L Z E F P M H J Z W O L A D P F I
J J T P D S Y I E H R I C V Z M N K Y W
J H S R G F Q D C G F R Z D B U W F A R
N H H U W J Q T X S P I F Z O G L P S X
O T T C Y E F J S H E C F G B D E E U R
R S U U C J I Q G C O M P A S S R O S E
T E Y T O K A O I N O V F Y A G R R Z F
H W L W C S X P W W U Q V W D P F F V Q
B B L U U M P B A W N O Z X W D T Q V Z
```

DESIGN A LICENSE PLATE

When drivers go to the Washington Department of Licensing to get license plates for their cars, they have a few designs to choose from. One plate design says "Evergreen State." Other designs highlight Washington's wildlife, lighthouses, and national parks. Imagine that you have been asked to come up with three new designs for Washington State license plates. Think of new, creative ways to represent the state. Sketch your ideas here!

GEOGRAPHY & SOCIAL STUDIES

A MAP BY ANY OTHER NAME . . . WOULD STILL BE A MAP

No doubt, you've heard the saying, "A picture is worth a thousand words." Maps are like pictures. They tell us a lot with very few words. Maps are important tools of geography, and they have many purposes.

Although different kinds of maps are designed to share different types of information, maps usually have common features like a title, a compass rose, a scale of miles, a legend (or key) to explain what symbols mean, and a grid. Study this map of Washington to answer the questions.

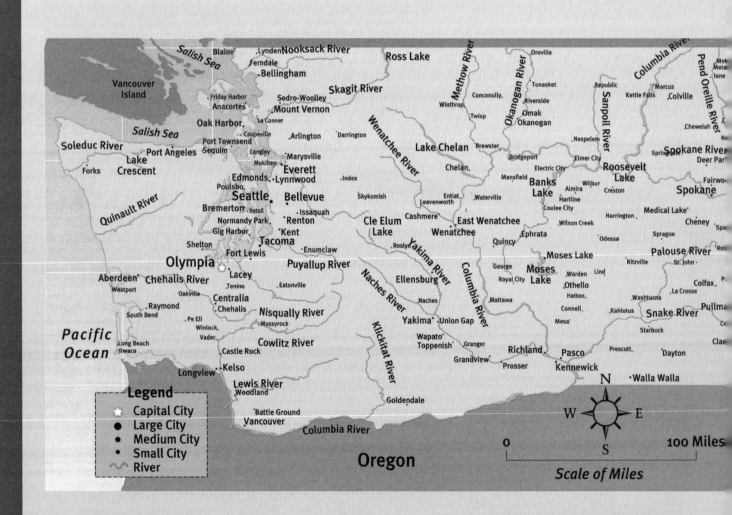

Legend
- ☆ Capital City
- ● Large City
- ● Medium City
- · Small City
- ∿ River

1. What does the legend (key) for this map tell us?

_____

_____

_____

2. What title would you give to this map?

_____

3. What is the capital city?

_____

Write at least three things that you learned from this map.

Hints: Did you learn anything new about Washington's cities and waterways? What does the map tell us about the city where you live?

_____

_____

_____

_____

_____

_____

_____

CREATE A CHALK MAP OF YOUR HOME

Go outside and find a large cement area where you can safely complete this activity. Using sidewalk chalk, create a map of your home and yard that a visitor could use to find his or her way around. Include each room inside your house. Also include the outdoor areas surrounding your home. Be sure to give your map a title and a legend. Don't forget to include a compass!

Before you start drawing, make a list of important things to include on your map. Then, decide on a symbol for each thing. Draw the symbols on the map and in the legend.

ITEM	SYMBOL

FIELD TRIP: SEE A BIG CITY

Washington State has an estimated population of 7,061,530 people who live in cities large and small. If you visit www.quickfacts.census.gov/qfd/states/53000.html, you can learn many interesting things about the residents of our amazing state. You can also select a specific county or a city in Washington to study. Is your city or town listed? Circle: YES or NO

Look at the quick facts about your city or town. List three new things you learned:

_____

_____

_____

Now choose a BIG city to visit. This website lists Washington's 11 major cities. www.citypopulation.de/php/usa-cenus-washington.php Which one is nearest where you live?

_____

With the help of an adult, research this city online and plan a field trip to visit a major attraction. For example, here's a list of the Top Ten Things to See in Seattle: www.10best.com/destinations/washington/seattle/attractions/best-attractions-activities/

What city did you visit?

_____

How far is it from where you live?

_____

What attraction did you see?

_____

What did you like most?

_____

POPULATION MAP OF WASHINGTON

This map shows the population of Washington's counties based on the 2010 census. Study the map and answer the questions.

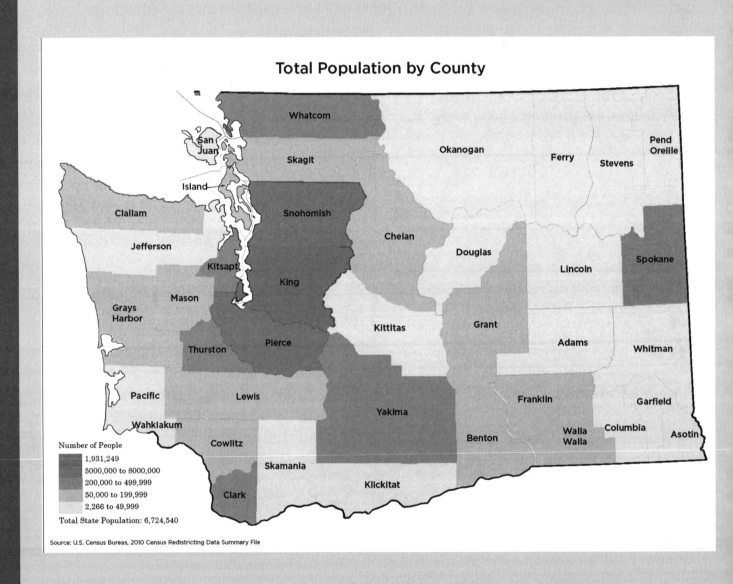

Total Population by County

Number of People
- 1,931,249
- 5000,000 to 8000,000
- 200,000 to 499,999
- 50,000 to 199,999
- 2,266 to 49,999

Total State Population: 6,724,540

Source: U.S. Census Bureas, 2010 Census Redistricting Data Summary File

1. How can you tell the difference in population between counties?

_____

2. Which county has the highest population?

_____

3. How would you describe the region of Washington that has the highest population?

_____

_____

_____

4. How would you describe the region of Washington that has the lowest population?

_____

_____

_____

5. Which three counties have the highest populations?

_____

_____

_____

6. Name five of the counties with the lowest populations.

_____

_____

_____

_____

7. Why do you think the population centers are around Puget Sound?

_____

_____

_____

8. What is the population like where you live? Are you surprised to see how your county's population compares to the rest of the state? Why or why not?

_____

_____

_____

_____

_____

_____

IMPORTANT PLACES IN WASHINGTON

Can you label each of these important places in Washington? Circle any of these places that you've visited.

COLUMBIA RIVER   OLYMPIA   SEATTLE   FORT VANCOUVER   SAN JUAN ISLANDS
VANCOUVER ISLAND   PUGET SOUND   PACIFIC OCEAN

LAND FEATURES CROSSWORD

Using the clues, solve the puzzle. If you need a hint, see the terms on the following page.

Across
6. large raised areas of mostly flat land
8. an area of land that has water on three sides

Down
1. high landforms with large bases and small peaks

2. small or narrow bays
3. a piece of land that juts out into a large body of water
4. areas that are usually soaked with water
5. a piece of land surrounded by water
7. a sheltered part of a body of water that is deep enough for anchoring ships

LAND FEATURES

Read about each of the landforms found in Washington. Then label each landform on the diagram. Do you have any of these landforms near your home? Circle them.

1. **Mountains** are high landforms with large bases and small peaks. A long line of mountains is called a mountain range. Washington is divided from east to west by the high Cascade Mountains. The Olympic Mountains are near the ocean.

2. A **Valley** is a low, flat land surrounded by mountains or plateaus. Cities, towns, and farms are often located in valleys.

3. A **foothill** is a low hill at the base of a mountain.

4. **Plateaus** are large raised areas of mostly flat land. Most of the eastern part of our state is on a plateau that was formed by flowing lava.

5. **Wetlands** are areas that are usually soaked with water.

6. A **harbor** is a sheltered part of a body of water that is deep enough for anchoring ships.

7. A **peninsula** is an area of land that has water on three sides.

8. **Inlets** are small or narrow bays.

9. **Rivers** and **streams** run down to the valleys, providing water for people and farms.

10. A **cape** is a piece of land that juts out into a large body of water.

11. An **island** is a piece of land surrounded by water on all sides. The San Juan Islands are beautiful places to visit by boat.

12. A **strait** is a narrow stretch of water between larger bodies of water.

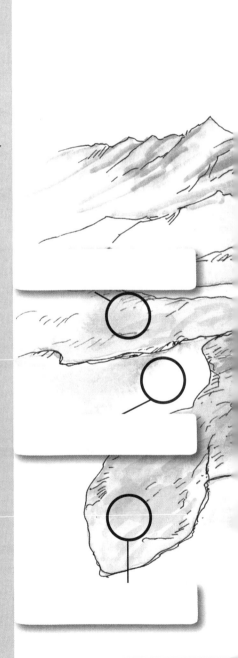

GEOGRAPHY & SOCIAL STUDIES

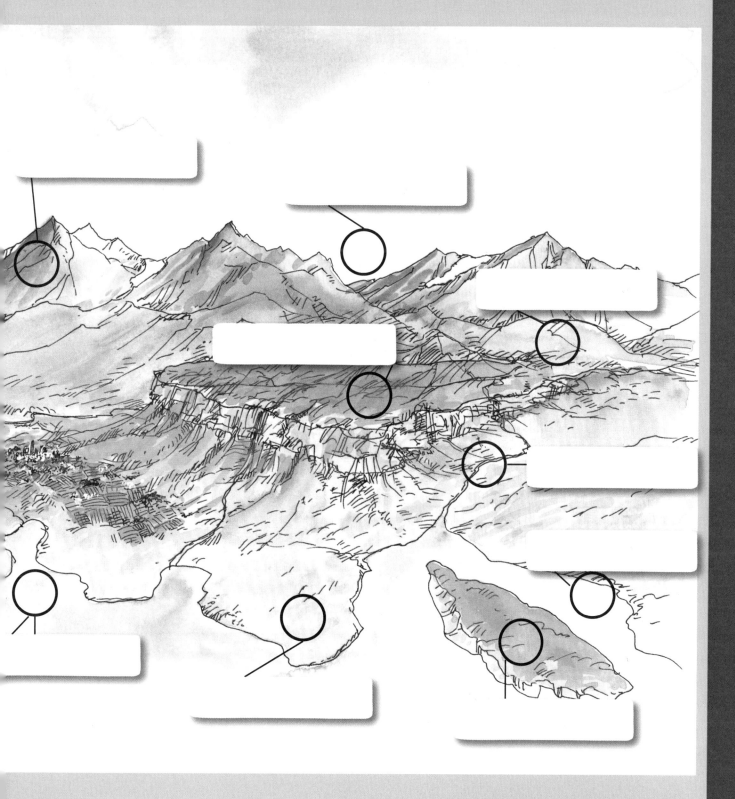

RELIEF MAP

In geography, the term relief refers to the elevation of the land, or how high above sea level an area is located. Below is a relief map of Washington. Notice how its different colors represent different elevations.

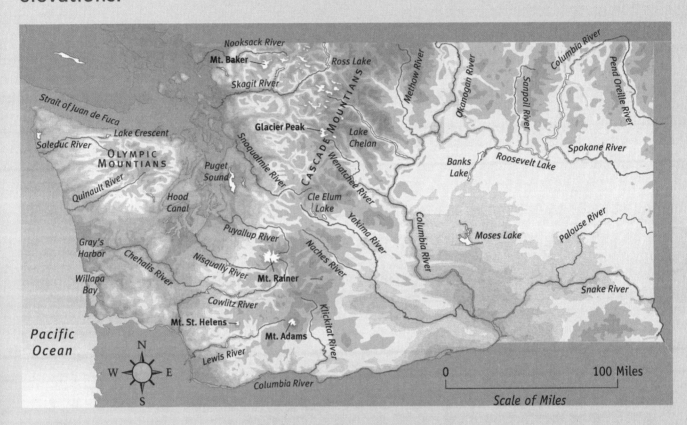

1. How do the colors help you understand the changes in elevation across our state?

_____

2. Which color represents the lowest elevations?

_____

3. Which color represents the highest elevations?

_____

4. Where are the areas with the lowest elevations found?

_____

5. Where are the areas with the highest elevations found?

_____

GEOGRAPHY & SOCIAL STUDIES

Now it's time for some hands-on fun! Use salt dough to create your own relief map of Washington. With the help of an adult, follow this recipe to make your own salt dough. Photocopy the map and place it on a cookie sheet. Using the relief map on the previous page as your guide, form your dough and place it on the map to create the high, low, and in-between elevations in Washington.

Salt Dough Recipe

4 CUPS FLOUR
1 CUP SALT
1 CUP HOT WATER
2 TEASPOONS VEGETABLE OIL

Stir flour and salt together. Slowly add water and oil. If the dough is sticky, add more flour. If it doesn't stick together well, add more water. Knead well.

PICTURING WASHINGTON'S LAND REGIONS

Do you remember how many land regions there are in Washington? Hold up your hand and spread your fingers wide. You've got it! The answer is five! Each region is defined by its most common landform. Read about the prominent features of each land region. Then create your own illustrations.

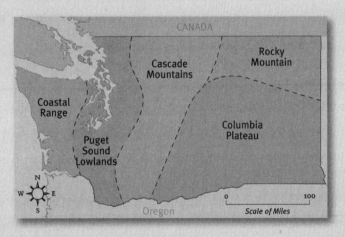

Coastal Range

Some parts of the coastline are rough and rocky. In other parts, you can walk along wide, sandy beaches. If you are on the coast, you won't have to travel far to see the towering, snowcapped Olympic Mountains. They are covered with thick forests. The ocean is an important natural resource in Washington.

Draw a picture of a scene from Washington's Coastal Range.

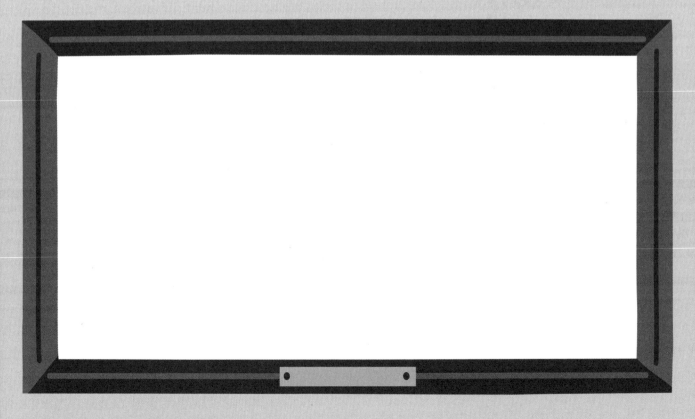

Puget Sound Lowlands

This region of valleys and low hills stretches out from the shores of Puget Sound. Miles of bays shape the coastline. Islands dot the water. The rolling ocean, flowing rivers, and rich farmland are valuable natural resources.

Draw a picture of a scene from Washington's Puget Sound Lowlands.

Cascade Mountains

The tall, rugged Cascade Mountains divide our state. There are five famous mountains in this region. They are Mt. Saint Helens, Mt. Rainier, Mt. Adams, Mt. Baker, and Glacier Peak. Forests of hemlock, fir, and cedar trees grow on the wet western side of the mountains. Their wood is an important natural resource.

Draw a picture of a scene from Washington's Cascade Mountains.

Columbia Plateau

On the east side of the Cascades is the wide, flat, plateau that covers most of eastern Washington. Large winding rivers are important, valuable resources. The Palouse is a farming region on the plateau. Palouse soil was formed thousands of years ago from volcanic ash and dust. The soil is this region's most valuable natural resource.

Draw a picture of a scene from Washington's Columbia Plateau.

Rocky Mountain Region

This region lies at the foothills of the great Rocky Mountains. The Rockies are the largest mountain range in North America. Forests are a natural resource that cover some of the highlands. Grazing land is also a rich resource.

Draw a picture of a scene from Washington's Rocky Mountain region.

FIELD TRIP: COAST TO THE COAST

Washington's Coastal Region is a great place to visit. From museums, to go-carts, to whale watching, there are many exciting things to do!

With the help of an adult, research activities in coastal Washington, and plan a family field trip. www.thingstodo.com/states/WA/coast.html.

If seeing Washington's beautiful beaches is on the top of your list, here are some websites to help you find the perfect shore.

Grays Harbor in the Southwest corner of the Olympic Peninsula
www.visitgraysharbor.com

Places to see on the North Coast
www.pbinn.com/northcoastattractions.htm

Washington's Long Beach Peninsula
www.funbeach.com

A picture is worth a thousand words! After your visit, draw what you saw at the seaside, or paste a picture of you enjoying your trip to the coast.

INDUSTRY MAP

Industry is all about the economy and how people make a living. Read about the various industries in each of Washington's regions. Use the information below to help you design an industry map of our state. First, create a legend for your map to represent Washington's main industries. For example, a fish could represent the fishing industry. Using the symbols you've created, fill each region with its appropriate industries.

Few people live in the **Coastal Range** region, so there are only a few small towns in this area. Some people in these towns earn money in the tourism industry, serving guests of the region's restaurants and hotels. Other people earn a living in the timber or fishing industries.

Large cities such as Seattle, Tacoma, Bellevue, Bremerton, Bellingham, Everett, and Olympia (the state Capital) make the **Puget Sound Lowlands** the population center of Washington State. People move here from many places in the world to work in different industries. Shipping is a major industry here. Many people make products to sell, such as airplanes, boats, and trucks. Tourism and agriculture are two more big industries in this region.

There are no large cities in the **Rocky Mountain Region**, but there are small towns and many ranches. To earn money in this rural region, people farm, raise cattle, cut timber, and mine lead and zinc.

There are no big cities in the steep mountains of the **Cascade Mountain Region**. However, Leavenworth is an example of the many smaller towns in the area that depend on tourism to sustain their economies. Another town, Ellensburg, has a university and a famous rodeo that brings in tourists from other towns and states. People also visit this region to hike, camp, fish, and ski. Other important industries in this region include forestry, agriculture, and creating electricity in dams.

The largest city in the **Columbia Plateau** is Spokane, which is a center for the healthcare industry. Pullman is a center of education and research. Washington State University is located here. Yakima and Wenatchee are centers for the fruit-growing industry. Smaller towns include the Tri-Cities of Richland, Pasco, and Kennewick. Agriculture is big business in the rural areas of this region.

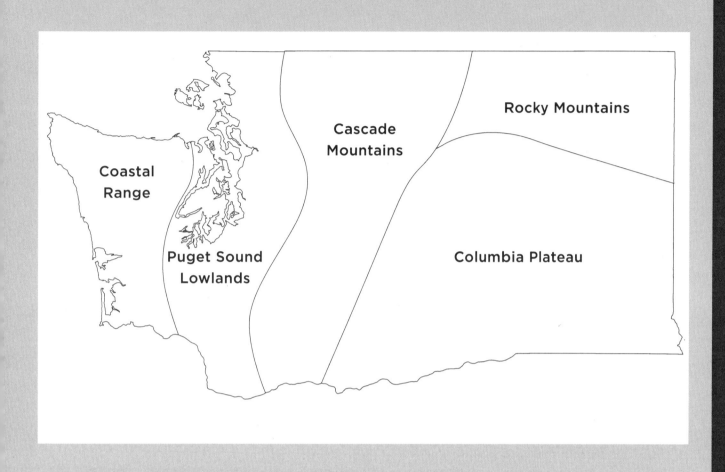

LEGEND			
ITEM	SYMBOL	ITEM	SYMBOL
TOURISM		HEALTHCARE	
TIMBER		EDUCATION	
FISHING		FORESTRY	
SHIPPING		HYDROELECTRICITY	
MANUFACTURING		EDUCATION	
AGRICULTURE		MINING	

NATIONAL PARKS

Washington is home to three national parks. The Mount Rainier, North Cascades, and Olympic National Parks can all be found in the western half of the state. Imagine that you are planning a family trip to see one of the parks. Use this page to help you plan the trip. Visit www.nps.gov to help you learn more about the parks. You can search for them by state or by name. Do some research about all three parks before choosing the one you want to plan this trip for.

We will be visiting

_____

National Park.

Date(s) of your visit:

_____

Distance to park:

_____

Amount of time needed to get to the park:

_____

Directions to the park:

_____

_____

_____

_____

Operating hours of the facilities during your visit:

_____

Available campground locations:

_____

_____

Where I want to camp:

_____

Different lengths of trails available:

_____

_____

_____

_____

Things to do at the park:

_____

_____

_____

_____

Nearby attractions:

_____

_____

_____

Likely weather conditions:

_____

Some history of the park:

_____

_____

_____

_____

Some details of the nature and
science of the park:

_____

_____

_____

_____

Fun things for kids to do in the park:

_____

_____

_____

Things I'm looking forward to most:

_____

_____

_____

FIELD TRIP: NATIONAL PARK

Turn your imaginary trip into a field trip! Make plans with your family to visit one of Washington's National Parks. If you aren't able to visit the park you chose in the last activity, is there another State or National Park you could see?

Use this website to learn more about Washington State Parks: www.parks.wa.gov

What park did you visit?

_____

When did you go?

_____

_____

What was the most interesting thing you saw?

_____

_____

_____

_____

What was the most fun thing you did?

_____

_____

_____

_____

_____

Draw a picture of you having fun!

GEOGRAPHY & SOCIAL STUDIES

TOURISM IN WASHINGTON

Tourism is a big industry in Washington State. People come here to visit our forests, mountains, coasts, monuments, and state and national parks.

At www.access.wa.gov/topics/visiting you can learn all about our office of tourism and many of the most popular tourist destinations in Washington. You can also go to www.experiencewa.com to learn about tourist attractions. These sites provide information to encourage people from around the world to visit Washington.

Imagine that you have just been asked by the governor's office to come up with a new slogan and ad campaign for the state tourism department. Write and design your slogan below. It should be short and catchy. You should design it to look appealing, too.

THIS IS ONLY A DRILL

Throughout its history, Washington has experienced many natural disasters. These include severe snowstorms, flooding, avalanches, volcano eruptions, forest fires, windstorms, and even tornadoes, just to name a few.

What if a natural disaster occurs near your home? The most important thing you can do to be prepared is to create a family plan of what to do in the event of an emergency. Use this planner to help your family put together an emergency plan.

Nearby emergency contact
(name and number):

_____

_____

Out-of-state emergency contact
(name and number):

_____

_____

Escape routes from each room in your home:

_____

_____

_____

_____

_____

Meeting place in the neighborhood
(if you can't enter your home):

_____

_____

Meeting place in the region
(if you can't enter your neighborhood):

_____

_____

Emergency phone numbers
(other than 9-1-1):

Fire:

_____

Police:

_____

Hospital:

_____

Insurance information:

_____

_____

Install and check smoke detectors.
Check your smoke detectors every six
months. Check them the same two dates
each year so it's easier to remember.
Family members' birthdays are always
a good time to do it.
Dates:

_____

Locations:

_____

Install and check fire extinguishers.
Check your fire extinguishers once a
year. Set the same date each year so it's
easier to remember.
Date:

_____

Locations:

_____

Keep a first-aid kit.
Location:

_____

CPR and other first-aid training:

_____

_____

Check furniture and items hanging on
the wall that could fall in an earthquake.
Secure the items to the wall.

Prepare 72-hour kits for each member
of the family, and have them in a place
you can easily get to them in the case of
an emergency. Change out food items in
your kits once a year. Set the same date
each year so it's easier to remember.
Date:

_____

Location:

_____

Have water containers filled and stored
in case of emergency. It is a good idea to
have large barrels to keep at your house
as well as smaller containers that you
could take with you if you have to leave.
Keep these near your 72-hour kits.
Location:

_____

It's a good idea to keep important
paperwork together in a safe place so
you could grab it and take it with you if
you needed to leave.

Revisit your emergency plan often.
Dates to revisit plan:

_____

Make sure everyone in your family has
a copy of the emergency information
with them. You might want to keep it in
the glove box of each car, in wallets, or
back packs.

PUT YOURSELF IN THE PICTURE

Some of the mountains in Washington are actually volcanoes, and some of the volcanoes are active! On May 18, 1980, Mt. Saint Helens erupted. This image shows what it looked like at one point during the eruption. Imagine looking out your window that day to see this scene. How would you have reacted? Write about what you might have thought, felt, or done at the sight of Mt. Saint Helens erupting.

View a Video
History.com has a 4-minute video you can watch about the eruption of Mt. Saint Helens. Visit this website to take a look: www.history.com/topics/us-states/washington/videos/mount-st-helens-erupts

PALEO-INDIANS

The first people to live here were Paleo-Indians. Paleo means ancient, or very old. Paleo-Indians lived all over the Americas. They hunted mammoths, mastodons, large wild cats, small horses, rabbits, antelope, and deer for food. They caught birds and fish. They gathered berries, nuts, seeds, and roots from plants. They didn't live in one place, but moved around to hunt and gather food. Compare how the Paleo-Indians lived to how you live today. In the left section, fill in details of how the Paleo-Indians lived. In the right section, fill in details of how you live. In the middle, fill in details that are the same for how both the Paleo-Indians and you live.

PALEO-INDIANS

BOTH

ME

ARCHAIC INDIANS

As the climate changed, so did the people's way of life. The people who lived during this time are called Archaic Indians. Archaic means old. Many of the giant animals no longer lived on the Earth. The people hunted deer and birds for food. They made new tools that allowed them to hunt smaller, faster animals. They also began to plant crops because they didn't move around as much as the people before them. To store the food for winter, they dug pits in the ground. Compare how the Archaic Indians lived to how you live today. In the left section, fill in details of how the Archaic Indians lived. In the right, fill in details of how you live. In the middle, fill in details that are the same for how both the Archaic Indians and you live.

ARCHAIC INDIANS

BOTH

ME

ARCHAIC AND PALEO-INDIANS

You know how your way of life compares to those who lived here long ago. But how do two groups from long ago compare to one another? Compare how the Paleo-Indians lived with how the Archaic Indians lived. In the left section, fill in details of how the Paleo-Indians lived. In the right section, fill in details of how the Archaic Indians lived. In the middle section, fill in details that are the same for both groups.

PALEO-INDIANS

BOTH

ARCHAIC INDIANS

What were some of the major differences between the two groups?

_____

_____

_____

MAKE YOUR OWN ROCK ART

Native American rock carvings are called petroglyphs. You can make your very own rock art with just a few ingredients from the craft store and the help of an adult.

WHAT YOU WILL NEED:

plaster
cookie sheet
wax paper
spatula
dark orange craft paint
paper clips

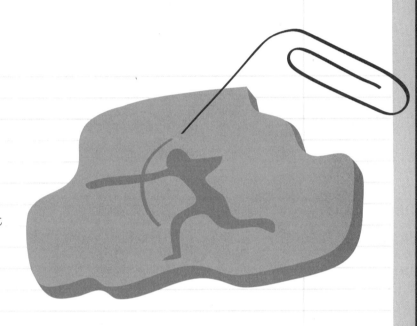

WHAT TO DO:

1. Mix the plaster, following the instructions on the package.

2. Line your cookie sheet with wax paper.

3. Poor the plaster into the cookie sheet. Use a flat spatula to spread it out on the cookie sheet. Let the plaster dry overnight.

4. Paint the entire surface of the plaster with a color similar to that of red sandstone rocks. Let the paint dry a few hours.

5. Have an adult use a blunt object, such as a butter knife, to break up the plaster into smaller pieces to make rocks.

6. Unwind the end of a paper clip. Use the end to carve symbols into your rocks. What story will you tell with your rock art?

7. Share your rock art with others to see if they can guess the meaning of your symbols.

INDIAN TRIBAL LANDS

This map shows Indian reservation lands in Washington during the 1800s.

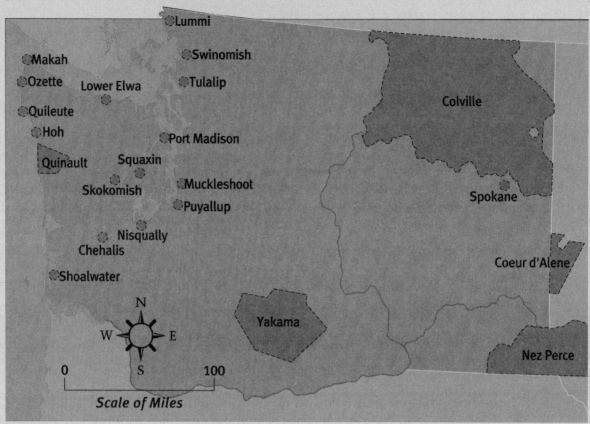

1. According to the map, which tribes seem to have the most land on their reservations?

_____

2. How would you describe where most of the tribes and reservations are located?

_____

3. Why do you think so many tribes are located near the coast or near water?

_____

_____

4. How might life on the Colville and Yakama reservations be different from life for the tribes along the coast?

_____

_____

_____

5. Are there any reservations near where you live? Which ones are closest?

_____

_____

NATURAL DYES

The first people to live in Washington, the American Indians, lived off of the earth. They found many uses for plants. One of the uses was using plants to dye string, cloth, and other things. You can try using plants as dyes with the help of an adult. Here is a list of some plants you can use and how long to boil each in a pot of water before you can use it as a dye. Try this out on some string or a small piece of cloth. If it works well, you may want to try it on some other items.

Sample list of dyes and sources:

Barks: Boil one hour
BROWN—ash, birch, walnut, maple
BLACK—alder
GOLD—eucalyptus
RED—bayberry

Twigs and Leaves: Boil two hours
GRAY—blackberry plant
YELLOW—poplar leaves, peach leaves
LIME GREEN—lily of the valley leaves

Vegetables and Berries: Boil 45 minutes
RED—raspberries, beets, strawberries
BLUE—blueberries, boysenberries
YELLOW—onion skin
GREEN—spinach, squash
BROWN—coffee grounds
ORANGE—carrots

Flowers: Boil 15 minutes
GREEN—morning glory
BEIGE—red bougainvillea
BLUE—cornflower, larkspur
RED—bloodroot poppy
YELLOW—goldenrod, dahlia, marguerite

PRESERVING MEAT

Salmon was the most important source of food for the Coastal Indians who lived along the coast of Washington. To make it last longer, they smoked and dried the fish to make it into a jerky-like meat. They did this by cutting the fish, cleaning it, removing the bones, and hanging it on wooden racks over smoky fires. The fish they caught and dried one season would last until it was time for the next salmon-fishing season. With the help of an adult, you can make your own jerky!

Ingredients:
LEAN MEAT AND SEASONING SALT

Directions:
1. Put the meat in the freezer until partially frozen. Partially frozen meat is easier to slice.

2. Slice meat thinly along the grain. Remove any visible fat.

3. Lay sliced meat on wax paper and sprinkle with seasoning salt. Work seasoning into the meat.

4. Put seasoned meat on a cookie sheet and place in the oven. Set oven temperature to 150 degrees. Cook for 5 hours. Leave the oven door slightly open to allow the water that is released from the meat to escape.

5. Allow the cooked meat to sit overnight before eating.

LEWIS AND CLARK'S JOURNEY

In 1803, the United States bought land from France. This area was known as the Louisiana Purchase, and it reached west from the Mississippi River to the Rocky Mountains. Because this land hadn't been explored much by Americans, the president of the asked Meriwether Lewis and William Clark to lead an expedition to learn more about the area. Study the map of the route followed by Lewis and Clark. Use the information on the map to help you answer the questions.

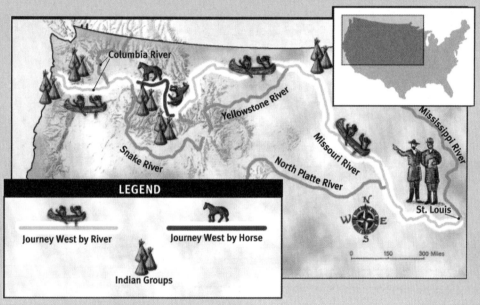

1. Where does the trail begin? _____

2. What rivers did the men follow? _____

3. What do you notice about the land where the explorers traveled by river?

_____

4. What do you notice about the land where the explorers traveled by horse?

_____

5. Where does the trail appear to end? _____

6. What dangers might the explorers have encountered on their journey west?

_____

LEWIS AND CLARK TIMELINE

This timeline shows the path the Lewis and Clark Expedition followed. It also provides notes from their journey and details about important events. Study the timeline and answer the questions.

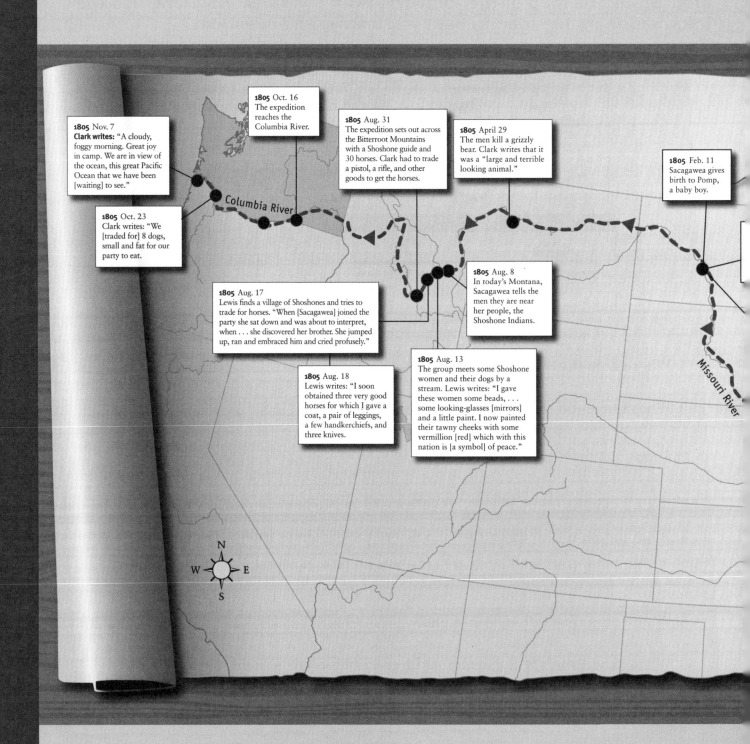

1805 Nov. 7
Clark writes: "A cloudy, foggy morning. Great joy in camp. We are in view of the ocean, this great Pacific Ocean that we have been [waiting] to see."

1805 Oct. 16
The expedition reaches the Columbia River.

1805 Aug. 31
The expedition sets out across the Bitterroot Mountains with a Shoshone guide and 30 horses. Clark had to trade a pistol, a rifle, and other goods to get the horses.

1805 April 29
The men kill a grizzly bear. Clark writes that it was a "large and terrible looking animal."

1805 Feb. 11
Sacagawea gives birth to Pomp, a baby boy.

1805 Oct. 23
Clark writes: "We [traded for] 8 dogs, small and fat for our party to eat.

1805 Aug. 8
In today's Montana, Sacagawea tells the men they are near her people, the Shoshone Indians.

1805 Aug. 17
Lewis finds a village of Shoshones and tries to trade for horses. "When [Sacagawea] joined the party she sat down and was about to interpret, when . . . she discovered her brother. She jumped up, ran and embraced him and cried profusely."

1805 Aug. 18
Lewis writes: "I soon obtained three very good horses for which I gave a coat, a pair of leggings, a few handkerchiefs, and three knives.

1805 Aug. 13
The group meets some Shoshone women and their dogs by a stream. Lewis writes: "I gave these women some beads, . . . some looking-glasses [mirrors] and a little paint. I now painted their tawny cheeks with some vermillion [red] which with this nation is [a symbol] of peace."

Columbia River

Missouri River

N
W   E
S

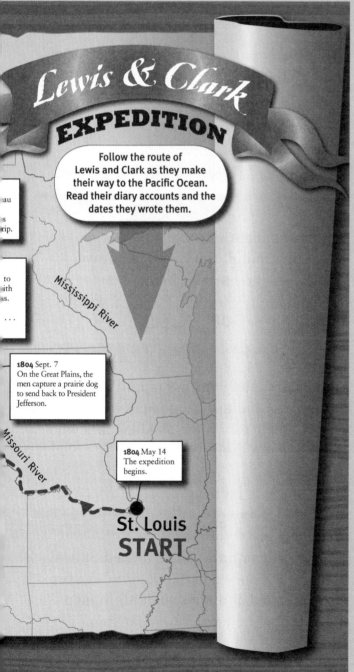

Lewis & Clark EXPEDITION

Follow the route of Lewis and Clark as they make their way to the Pacific Ocean. Read their diary accounts and the dates they wrote them.

Mississippi River

Missouri River

1804 Sept. 7
On the Great Plains, the men capture a prairie dog to send back to President Jefferson.

1804 May 14
The expedition begins.

St. Louis
START

When did the expedition begin?

_____

About how long did the men travel before they stopped for the winter?

_____

What event took place on April 29, 1805?

_____

To what tribe of Indians did Sacagawea belong?

_____

What happy discovery was made in August among the Shoshone Indians?

_____

When did the expedition reach the Columbia River?

_____

What unusual thing did the men eat while traveling along the Columbia River?

_____

What was the weather like when the men reached the Pacific Ocean?

_____

FACT OR FICTION?

Some books refer to mountain men as daring, tough adventurers. These books say that Washington's early explorers fought Indians and bears at every turn . . . but that is only partly true. Can you separate fact from fiction about mountain men? Take your best guess at which of these statements about mountain men are true.

Many mountain men were married, some to Indian women.

TRUE   FALSE

Their wives and families did not travel with them.

TRUE   FALSE

Most trapped for only a few years. Then they became guides, ranchers, farmers, or store owners.

TRUE   FALSE

They traveled by horse, mule, or canoe.

TRUE   FALSE

Most died from attack by wild animals.

TRUE   FALSE

Trapping was a hobby. Trappers did it purely for the excitement.

TRUE   FALSE

Mountain men were the best of the best all around. They were all brave, creative, and hardworking.

TRUE   FALSE

They often did not understand American Indians. Instead of respecting them, some saw them as nuisances who were just in their way.

TRUE   FALSE

When beaver hats in the United States and in Europe went out of style, the fur trade ended and many mountain men had to find new ways to make money.

TRUE   FALSE

COMPARING MAPS

These maps show the changes to the Washington and Oregon Territories during the mid-1800s. Answer the questions about these changes.

Territories 1853

CANADA
0
250 Miles
WASHINGTON TERRITORY
OREGON TERRITORY
N W E S

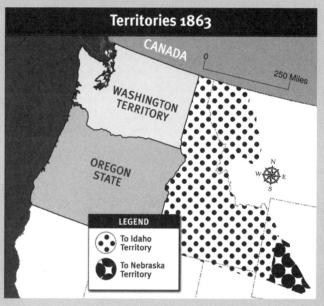

Territories 1863

CANADA
0
250 Miles
WASHINGTON TERRITORY
OREGON STATE
N W E S

LEGEND
To Idaho Territory
To Nebraska Territory

1. What regions are shown on the map from 1853?

_____

2. How did Washington Territory change from 1853 and 1863?

_____

3. What happened to Oregon Territory between 1853 and 1863?

_____

4. What territories existed in the region in 1863?

_____

5. How are the boundaries of Washington Territory in 1853 similar to the boundaries of Washington State today? How are they different?

_____

_____

THE PIG WAR

This map shows the San Juan Islands, a group of three islands that both the British and the Americans wanted to own. The dashed lines on the map illustrate different ways the countries thought the islands should be divided. This conflict over land ownership lead to the Pig War in 1859, where the only life lost was that of one pig.

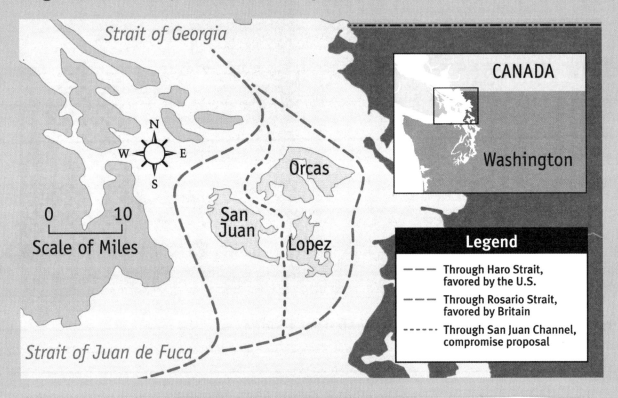

1. What is shown on the map?

_____

2. Why do you think the United States favored a boundary line through the Haro Strait?

_____

3. Do you agree with the idea of settling by dividing the islands through the San Juan Channel?

_____

4. Why or Why not?

_____

ACT IT OUT!

Here's your chance to bring history to life with a short skit. You can keep it simple OR add costumes, props, and scenery. Direct it however you'd like! You will need enough people for each of the following characters:

> A PIG
> A BRITISH SETTLER
> AN AMERICAN SETTLER
>
> A BRITISH CROWD
> AN AMERICAN CROWD
> THE RULER OF GERMANY

Pig: Oink, oink, I'm hungry! There sure are some delicious potatoes on that American settler's farm. I'm gonna eat some!

The pig eats the potatoes while the settlers approach.

American Settler: Hey! Keep your pig on your own land!

British Settler: What's the big deal? It's just a pig.

American Settler: Get your pig off my land NOW!

British Settler: Make me!

American Settler: You give me no choice.

American Settler shoots the pig. The pig dies.

British Settler: You just shot my pig! This means war!

British and American Crowds: (Chanting) Fight! Fight! Fight!

American Crowd: This land is ours!

British Crowd: No, it's not. It's ours!

British and American Crowds: (Chanting) This means war! This means war!

British Settler: Wait! Maybe there's another way. I'm sorry my pig ate your potatoes.

American Settler: Apology accepted. I'm sorry I shot your pig.

British Settler: Let's ask the ruler of Germany for help!

American Settler: That's a great idea.

British and American Crowds: Ruler of Germany, what should we do? Who should the San Juan Islands go to?

Ruler of Germany: I've heard both sides of your story. Here is my ruling. The United States has a stronger claim on this land. It belongs to the USA.

American Crowd: Cheers and high-fives.

British Crowd: Actors hang their heads and start to walk away.

American Crowd: The Pig War is over! No soldiers were lost.

Pig: One hungry pig was the war's only cost. Oink, oink!

FIND THE HIDDEN TERM

There are some special things in Washington, and some of them were even chosen by school children. Unscramble each of the clue words below and fill in the boxes next to the words. Copy the letters that have a number under them to the lines with the same numbers at the bottom of this page to find the hidden term.

WILLOW GOLDFINCH   WESTERN HEMLOCK   GREEN DARNER DRAGONFLY
COAST RHODODENDRON   STEELHEAD TROUT   APPLE
SQUARE DANCE   COLUMBIAN MAMMOTH

liwwol glcohfind

_ _ _ _ _ _   _ _ _ _ _ _ _ _ _
            10

rwseetn colhkme

_ _ _ _ _ _ _   _ _ _ _ _ _
    12 2

geern raedrn loarygfnd

_ _ _ _ _   _ _ _ _ _ _   _ _ _ _ _ _ _ _ _
      5   7

costa nedhodrodnor

_ _ _ _ _   _ _ _ _ _ _ _ _ _ _ _
     6

detselhea routt

_ _ _ _ _ _ _ _ _   _ _ _ _ _
       11   4

papel

_ _ _ _ _
1

saeruq nacde

_ _ _ _ _ _   _ _ _ _ _
1

biamocnul maohtmm

_ _ _ _ _ _ _ _ _   _ _ _ _ _ _ _
       8 9

_ _ _ _ _ _   _ _ _ _ _ _ _
1 2 3 4 5   6 7 8 9 10 11 12

GEOGRAPHY & SOCIAL STUDIES

FAVORITE STATE SYMBOLS

Have an adult help you do an Internet search about Washington's state symbols. Choose four of them that you find the most interesting. Write down each symbol you chose and three facts about each one. Then, draw a picture of each symbol.

SYMBOL: _____

Fact 1: _____

Fact 2: _____

Fact 3: _____

SYMBOL: _____

Fact 1: _____

Fact 2: _____

Fact 3: _____

SYMBOL: _____

Fact 1: _____

Fact 2: _____

Fact 3: _____

SYMBOL: _____

Fact 1: _____

Fact 2: _____

Fact 3: _____

READING & WRITING

130 Namesake

132 Land Metaphors

134 A Washington Portrait

136 Three Types of Communities

139 Field Trip: Space Needle

140 I Looked Out My Window

141 Home, Sweet Home

142 Hear, Hear! This Is the Best!

146 This Is Our Place!

147 My Favorite Place!

148 Help Wanted Ads

150 The View from Here

151 Put Some Paint On It!

152 Tanka Poem: My City

154 Cite Text Evidence: Mt. Saint Helens

156 Pacific Rim

158 Archaic Tools

160 Nuts About Nuts!

161 A Legend Online

162 Legends

164 The Great Debate: The Makah Whale Hunt

166 The Great Makah Word Hunt

167 A Snack for a Sailor

168 Early Explorers to the Pacific Northwest: The Spanish

172 Early Explorers to the Pacific Northwest: The English

174 Early Explorers to the Pacific Northwest: The Americans

176 You're Hired!

177 The Fur Trade Maze

178 Lewis and Clark Limerick

179 "Wheel" You Please Draw Some Pictures?

180 A Day in the Life of an Explorer

182 What Can You See in the Sea?

183 Campfires

184 Settlers and Indians

185 Field Trip: Native American Heritage

NAMESAKE

If Washington's lakes and rivers could talk, they would have many stories to tell. Each place and land feature in Washington has a story behind its name. The Yakima River gets its name from the Yakama Nation. Fort Lewis is named after Meriwether Lewis of the Lewis and Clark Expedition. The city of Seattle and Moses Lake were named after American Indian leaders. Olympia was once known by the natives as Cheetwoot, which meant the "place of the bear," and was named Olympia by settlers in the Olympic Mountains. Tacoma is a Lushootseed Indian word meaning "snow-covered mountain."

What about you? What is your namesake, or where did your name come from? Write an informative paragraph sharing the history of your name.

CHALLENGE!

TOPIC SENTENCE: Explain that you will be sharing where your name came from.

_____

SUPPORTING SENTENCE 1: Begin explaining your namesake.

_____

SUPPORTING SENTENCE 2: More information on your namesake.

_____

SUPPORTING SENTENCE 3: More information on your namesake.

_____

CONCLUDING SENTENCE: Restate and wrap up the purpose of the paragraph.

_____

Do you have more to say about your name? Use the information from the previous page as an introductory paragraph and continue working on a five-paragraph essay. Tell as much as you can about your namesake.

INTRODUCTORY PARAGRAPH

_____
_____
_____
_____

SUPPORTING DETAILS
(USE SUPPORTING SENTENCE 1)

_____
_____
_____
_____
_____

SUPPORTING DETAILS
(USE SUPPORTING SENTENCE 2)

_____
_____
_____
_____
_____

SUPPORTING DETAILS
(USE SUPPORTING SENTENCE 3)

_____
_____
_____
_____
_____

CONCLUDING PARAGRAPH

_____
_____
_____
_____

LAND METAPHORS

A metaphor is a word or phrase for one thing that is used to refer to another thing. Writers use metaphors to add emotion and feeling. One writer, Barry Lopez, wrote,

"To put your hands in a river is to feel the chords that bind the earth together."

His metaphor relates rivers to chords. A chord is three or more musical tones sounded at the same time. His metaphor paints an image in our minds of rivers all around the world playing musical notes together, their beautiful music binding the earth.

Think of a time you spent outdoors in Washington. What land feature stuck out most to you? Choose one of the land features below and use a metaphor to write a sentence or two describing the feature. What will you relate the landform to in your metaphor?

MOUNTAIN	VALLEY	PLATEAU	FOOTHILL	WETLAND	HARBOR
PENINSULA	INLET	CAPE	ISLAND	STRAIT	

_____

_____

_____

_____

Can you think of second land feature metaphor?

_____

_____

_____

Show how you visualize your metaphors by drawing pictures of the land features you described.

A WASHINGTON PORTRAIT

Washington is a state of many stories. One of the most important stories you'll be involved in is your own! How long have you lived in Washington? What matters most to you about living here? What do you want to accomplish as a resident of this great state? Paint a picture with words as you create your own Washington Portrait. Think back on memorable events in your life history, look ahead to the future, and tell your personal story. Use this organizer to help you. Review and revise your rough draft. Then, rewrite your "polished" story on the next page.

Where?

_____

When?

_____

Who?

_____

Situation

_____

_____

Event #1

_____

_____

Event #2

_____

_____

Event #3

_____

_____

Conclusion

_____

_____

WASHINGTON PORTRAIT

NAME

YEAR I WAS BORN

THREE TYPES OF COMMUNITIES

You can find three kinds of communities in Washington State: rural, suburban, and urban. Read about each kind of community and answer the questions that follow.

Urban Communities

Cities are busy places. They have sidewalks full of people. The streets are noisy with cars. There are houses, apartments, and rows of businesses. This kind of community is called an urban community. People in urban areas often walk or ride buses or trains to get from place to place. Washington's most urban area is Seattle.

Suburban Communities

Some people like to live outside the city. There, the houses and businesses are more spread out than in urban communities. There are parks and lawns to play on. These areas are called suburban communities, or suburbs.

Many people work in the cities but live in the suburbs. They drive or take commuter trains to work. To commute means to travel some distance between home and work. Suburbs are often built on land that was once farmland. Some popular suburban areas near Seattle are Bellevue, New Castle, Redmond, Bothell, Kenmore, and Renton.

Rural Communities

Some people live in small towns or on farms in the country. Farmers need plenty of land on which to grow crops and use as pasture for their livestock. This kind of open land is rural. Rural areas look very different from urban areas.

Most Washingtonians live in urban areas and suburbs, but some prefer living in the country!

READING & WRITING

Do you live in an urban, suburban, or rural community? Draw a picture of where you live. Then write a descriptive paragraph about what type of community you live in. Include details that make it urban, suburban, or rural. Use the lines below to form your ideas and then write your paragraph on the next page.

MY COMMUNITY

TOPIC SENTENCE: State which type or community you live in and give your city or town name.

_____

SUPPORTING SENTENCE 1: Describe one of your city/town's traits that make that type of community.

_____

SUPPORTING SENTENCE 2: Describe another of your city/town's traits that make that type of community.

_____

SUPPORTING SENTENCE 3: Describe one more of your city/town's traits that make that type of community.

_____

CONCLUDING SENTENCE: Restate which kind of community you live in.

_____

MY COMMUNITY

FIELD TRIP: SPACE NEEDLE

Located in downtown Seattle, the Space Needle is one of Washington's most famous urban landmarks. With the help of an adult, visit www.spaceneedle.com and plan a trip to see this amazing structure.

If a field trip isn't possible, take a virtual tour of the Space Needle. Visit www.spaceneedle.com/fun-facts to learn more. Get a "needle-eye view" by checking out the Space Needle's webcam (www.spaceneedle.com/webcam)!

It is really cool looking down from so high up in the air! Things on the ground look so small. Make a list of five things you can see.

_____

_____

_____

_____

_____

How did you feel about being so far above the ground?

_____

_____

_____

_____

_____

I LOOKED OUT MY WINDOW

Take a look out of your bedroom window. What do you see? First, draw a close-up picture of what's right outside the window. Then, draw a picture of what you can see in the distance.

WHAT I SEE CLOSE UP

WHAT I SEE FARTHER AWAY

HOME, SWEET HOME

What makes your house unique? Explore your home and notice what makes it special. What are three things a visitor might find most interesting?

_____

_____

_____

Draw a picture of your house.

HEAR, HEAR! THIS IS THE BEST!

An opinion is a belief or way of thinking about something. When good writers share their opinions, they have good reasons to support or explain them. Let's practice writing an opinion with supporting reasons.

In your opinion, which type of community is the best to live in: rural, suburban, or urban? Use this organizer to help you organize your ideas. In this step of the writing process, we are just organizing ideas, not using complete sentences yet; words or phrases are okay to use here.

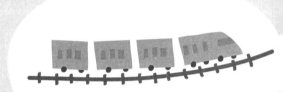

INTRODUCTION

Answer to the question:

Three supporting reasons:

REASON #1	REASON #2	REASON #3
SUPPORTING DETAIL	SUPPORTING DETAIL	SUPPORTING DETAIL
SUPPORTING DETAIL	SUPPORTING DETAIL	SUPPORTING DETAIL
SUPPORTING DETAIL	SUPPORTING DETAIL	SUPPORTING DETAIL

CONCLUSION

Restate your answer to the question:

Revisit each of your reasons:

Wrap it up with a final statement:

PARAGRAPH 1: This paragraph will be about five sentences. For your first sentence, restate the question as a statement and give your answer. For example, "I believe that suburbs make the best communities to live in." Each sentence after that should introduce one of your three reasons for your opinion.

_____

_____

_____

_____

PARAGRAPH 2: Your first sentence, topic sentence, will be your Reason #1. You should have about three sentences that follow, one for each of the supporting details.

_____

_____

_____

_____

PARAGRAPH 3: Your first sentence, topic sentence, will be your Reason #2. You should have about three sentences that follow, one for each of the supporting details.

_____

_____

_____

_____

PARAGRAPH 4: Your first sentence, topic sentence, will be your Reason #3. You should have about three sentences that follow, one for each of the supporting details.

_____

_____

_____

_____

_____

PARAGRAPH 5: This paragraph will be about five sentences. For your first sentence, you will again restate the question as a statement and give your answer. Each sentence after that should restate/revisit each of your reasons. Be careful not to introduce any new information here! Your last sentence should wrap up all of your writing.

_____

_____

_____

_____

_____

_____

_____

_____

THIS IS OUR PLACE!

People have a lot to think about when they decide where to live. Some common things people have to think about are where their job is located, where family is located, what the weather is like, what the land is like, and which type of community they want to live in. How did your family decide where to live? Use this page to help you research and write about how your family chose where to live.

Which type of community do you live in?

☐ SUBURBAN   ☐ URBAN   ☐ RURAL

Where did your family live before?

_____

Why did your family move from the previous location?

_____

Do you have family nearby?

_____

Where do your parents work?

_____

_____

Write a paragraph summarizing all of the reasons why your family chose to live where they do now. Your first sentence should be your topic sentence that introduces where your family lives now. You should write one sentence for each of the reasons why you live there. Your last sentence should wrap up your paragraph by restating where you live now.

_____

_____

_____

_____

_____

_____

MY FAVORITE PLACE!

Washington is full of wonderful places, from its rough and rocky coastline to the wide, flat Columbia Plateau. Where is your favorite place to visit in Washington? Describe your favorite place. Be sure to include details about where the place is, when you were last there, what you like to do there, and what it sounds like and looks like there. Write away!

Washington's natural resources make it a logical place for certain job industries. Fishing, shipping, agriculture, tourism, skiing, mining, and forestry are all big industries here.

Imagine that you work for a local newspaper and have been asked to write help wanted ads. Choose three industries that appeal most to you. Write an ad for each, telling all about the industry and enticing people to apply for the job. Include a catchy title and information about the kind of job that is available. If you need some ideas, look at the employment section of your newspaper, or at the website of your local paper and search for jobs.

HELP WANTED!

_____

_____

_____

_____

_____

HELP WANTED!

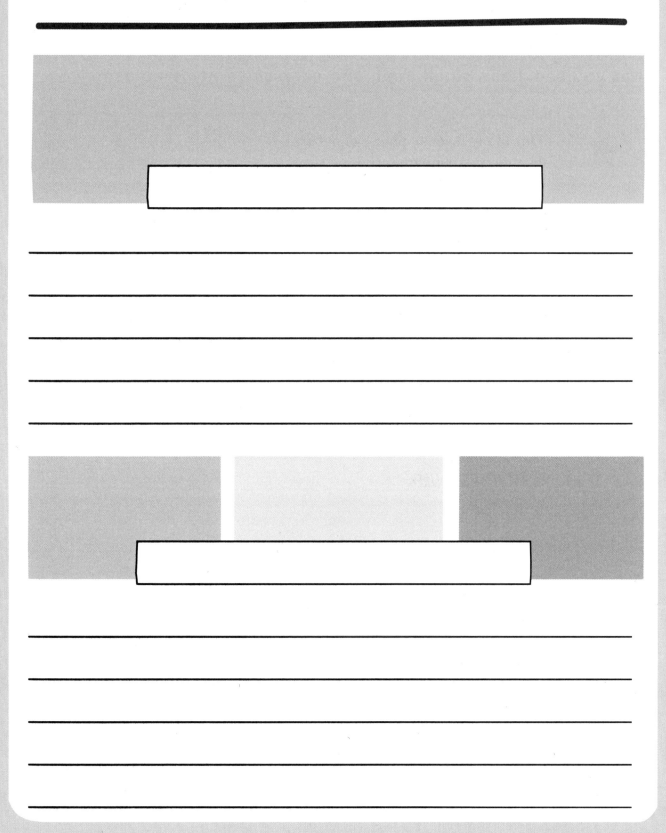

THE VIEW FROM HERE

Washington has many natural wonders and so much beauty. Write a description of one of your favorite natural beauties in Washington. It might be near your home, or it might be somewhere you have visited. A good description appeals to the senses. Be sure to write what you see, hear, smell, feel, and even taste at this place.

One of my favorite places of natural beauty in Washington is . . . _____

WHAT IT LOOKS LIKE

_____

WHAT IT SOUNDS LIKE

_____

WHAT IT SMELLS LIKE

_____

WHAT IT FEELS LIKE

_____

WHAT IT TASTES LIKE

_____

PUT SOME PAINT ON IT!

Here's a fun way to put some color on your favorite place!

YOU WILL NEED:

White drawing paper
Masking tape
Scissors
Paint

DIRECTIONS:

1. Carefully cut and place strips of tape to form each letter of your favorite place on the piece of paper.
2. Decorate the paper with paint, covering the entire surface. You don't need to worry about getting paint on the tape.
3. Once the paint is completely dry, carefully peel the tape off the paper. Work slowly so the paper doesn't tear.

TANKA POEM: MY CITY

Tanka poems are fun to write because they are short and simple. One Tanka poem has just five lines and thirty-one syllables total. There are five syllables in lines 1 and 3 and seven syllables in lines 2, 4, and 5.

Here is an example of a Tanka poem written about Washington State.

WASHINGTON REGIONS

THERE ARE FIVE REGIONS IN ALL

EACH ONE IS UNIQUE

SOME HAVE MOUNTAINS, SOME ARE FLAT

SOME ARE WET AND SOME ARE DRY

Write a Tanka poem about the place where you live. Include some of the most important features of your town or city.

TITLE: _____

Line 1: Five syllables _____

Line 2: Seven syllables _____

Line 3: Five syllables _____

Line 4: Seven syllables _____

Line 5: Seven syllables _____

Now that your poem is complete, memorize it and share it with a friend or family member.

CITE TEXT EVIDENCE: MT. SAINT HELENS

Washington is home to five active volcanoes. The most recent volcano eruption was in 1980, at Mt. Saint Helens. Read about the eruption of Mt. Saint Helens and then answer the questions that follow.

1. Mountains are very important landforms in Washington. Some of the mountains are actually volcanoes!

2. In early 1980, there were signs of danger on Mt. Saint Helens. Small earthquakes shook the land. Towers of smoke rose from the mountaintop. Scientists could tell that the mountain was swelling. Everyone living nearby was told to leave the area. Most people did. Still, no one knew exactly what might happen.

3. On May 18, the entire state of Washington found out. Mt. Saint Helens erupted! The force broke rocks into fine gray dust called ash. A fountain of ash shot nine miles into the sky. Wind blew the ash all across the state. The ash filled the sky and blocked the sun. In the middle of the day, some places were still as dark as night.

4. Highways, schools, and businesses closed. People had to stay indoors. Meanwhile, snow on the mountain melted. The melt-off mixed with dirt and formed gooey mud. Great rivers of mud, called mudslides, carried away houses and caused huge floods.

READING & WRITING

Did people have warnings that the volcano was going to erupt? In which paragraph did you find your answer? Begin your answer, "In paragraph ___ it said . . ."

_____

_____

_____

Describe the volcanic eruption. In which paragraph did you gather these details?

_____

_____

_____

Was everything okay once the volcano was done erupting? How do you know?

_____

_____

_____

What are some of the dangers of living near mountains in Washington?

_____

_____

_____

_____

PACIFIC RIM

An important reading skill to develop is the ability to reference and understand exactly what a passage of text said in order to answer related questions. Read this informational text about the Pacific Rim and then read the questions. Determine in which line or lines you'll find the answers to each question. Finally, answer the questions.

1. Find the Pacific Ocean on a globe or a world map. Then find Washington State in
2. North America and all the other countries that touch the Pacific Ocean. These lands
3. make up a large region called the Pacific Rim.
4. Japan, China, and Korea are countries in Asia. They lie along the Pacific Rim. The
5. United States and many other countries are part of the Pacific Rim, too.
6. Each day, hundreds of ships and airplanes travel back and forth between the cities
7. of the Pacific Rim. Visit a busy seaport in Washington, and you might see a ship
8. bringing cards from Japan. You might see Washington farm products being loaded
9. and shipped to China. You might see airplanes full of tourists and business people.
10. All of this selling and buying with people who live along the Pacific Rim is
11. important.
12. This is the way people get the things they want. This is also the way many
13. people earn money for their families.

LINE #

_____ What is the Pacific Rim?

_____

_____

_____ Name a few of the countries that are part of the Pacific Rim.

_____

_____

_____ What is the importance of the Pacific Rim?

_____

_____

_____

_____ Study the map of the Pacific Rim. Use information from the map and from the reading to draw two conclusions about the Pacific Rim.

_____

_____

_____

_____

_____

ARCHAIC TOOLS

The Archaic, or early, people of the world lived in North and South America between 8,000 BC and AD 200. Over time, they made better tools to help them hunt for and prepare food. Read about some of the ancient tools archaeologists have discovered. Then, answer the questions.

Axe

The Archaic people made axes of wood and stone.

Drills

A stone drill was attached to the end of a wooden rod. Rotating the rod turned the drill.

Atlatl

The Archaic people invented the atlatl to help them hunt animals that could run quickly like deer. The atlatl allowed the hunter to throw the spear with more force.

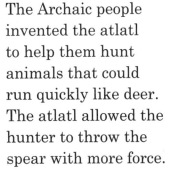

Bone pin   Needle

Bone Needles, Fishhooks, and Spear Points

The people made the bones of animals, especially deer, into fishhooks, needles, and spear points.

Grinding Stones

Archaic people pounded nut meat into flour using grinding stones called a mano and a metate. The mano was a small stone they pushed on a larger, flatter stone called a metate to grind the nuts.

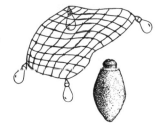

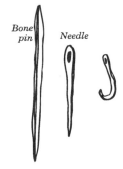

Fish Net Sinkers

Fish net sinkers were rocks that were used to weight a net and cause it to sink.

Circle the correct answer for the questions.

1. This reading describes tools archaeologists found that help them understand what group of early people?

A. Hohokam

B. Aztec

C. Archaic

D. Paleo-Indians

2. What did the Archaic people use the grinding stones for?"

A. Grinding stones were used to hunt small animals.

B. Grinding stones were used to grind nut meat into flour.

C. Grinding stones were used to grind small rocks to use as weapons.

D. Grinding stones were used to start a fire.

3. What was an atlatl?

A. An atlatl was a warrior who hunted for food.

B. An atlatl was a tool used to make baskets.

C. An atlatl was a tool made to help throw a spear faster and farther.

D. An atlatl was a longer and faster spear used to hunt small animals.

4. What was the main idea of this reading passage?

A. Archaic people lived long ago.

B. Archaic people liked to keep busy.

C. Archaic people ate many different kinds of foods.

D. Archaic people made many tools to hunt and prepare their food.

NUTS ABOUT NUTS!

Nuts and seeds were an important part of the Archaic people's diet. One of the tools they used, a set of stones called **nutting stones**, helped them grind up nuts and plants.

You can make your own nutting stones by finding a round rock that fits in the palm of your hand and a large, flat rock that you can pound on. Make sure you clean and dry your rocks well before you use them. Place nuts or seeds (shelled walnuts, almonds, peanuts, etc.) on the surface of the flat rock. Carefully pound them with the round rock until they are crushed into smaller pieces. Now you can add them to a salad, a cookie recipe, or even a smoothie!

A LEGEND ONLINE

With the permission of an adult, go online and enjoy this YouTube video of a Native American legend:

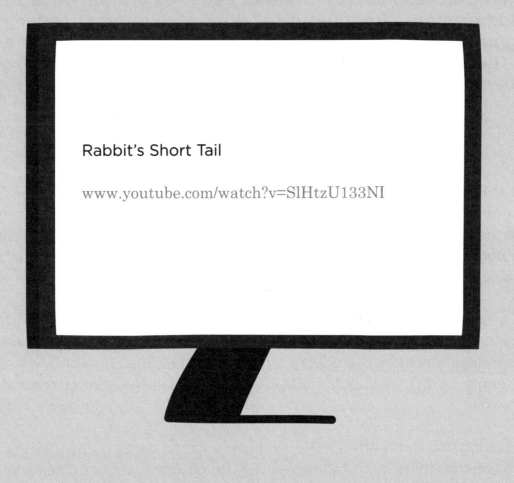

Rabbit's Short Tail

www.youtube.com/watch?v=SlHtzU133NI

Did you like this story? Why or why not?

_____

_____

_____

_____

What did you learn about the rabbit?

_____

_____

_____

LEGENDS

American Indian groups told legends as a way of explaining how something came to be. There is a legend to tell why the owl stays up late and how the land was created. Legends are fun because they include elements from nature and have an interesting way of explaining uninteresting things. There are many legends online and in books. The book, *Spider Spins a Story: Fourteen Legends from Native America*, by Jill Max was written for kids and is a great read.

Read this legend, "Why the Year Has 12 Months" to see if you can identify the elements of nature.

Why the Year Has 12 Months
It is winter, and you are tired of being inside. Your grandmother puts a few more sticks on the fire. She tells you and your brothers and sisters to come and sit around the fire. She begins to tell you a story. You listen closely. Someday you will tell this story to your own children.

Coyote and a large bird with 12 feathers in its tail were having an argument. They could not agree on how many months there should be in the year. Coyote said there should be as many months as there were hairs in his coat. The large bird, which was probably an eagle, said there should be as many months in the year as there were feathers in his tail.

After much talking, the bird ended it. He said there would be as many months in the year as there were feathers in his tail unless Coyote could catch him. Then the bird flew away. Because Coyote could not fly, he could not catch the bird. That is why there have been, to this day, 12 months in the year.

—adapted from a Goshute legend told by William Palmer in *Why the North Star Stands Still and Other Indian Legends*.

What elements of nature are in the legend?

_____

_____

_____

Now it's your turn to write a legend! Legends are short because they were passed down from person to person before people could read or write. Keep yours short enough to retell without having to read it.

What will you explain? (Examples: Why the sky is blue, why the night is dark, how babies learn to walk)

_____

What elements of nature will you use?

_____

Beginning: Introduce your characters and the problem.

_____

_____

_____

Middle: Tell the steps taken to solve the problem.

_____

_____

_____

End: Tell what the end result is. Include a statement like "And that's why . . ."

_____

_____

_____

THE GREAT DEBATE: THE MAKAH WHALE HUNT

The Makah Tribe began hunting whales over 4,000 years ago. All Washington tribes had hunting skills. The Makah, however, were one of the few tribes that hunted whales. Whale hunters prepared carefully. They took time to rest and pray for a safe and successful hunt. Only then did the hunters paddle out to the sea in large, beautifully carved canoes. When they spotted a whale, the hunt began.

There was no room for mistakes. One canoe came up close to the animal's left side. The chief hunter thrust his harpoon, or long spear, into the whale's huge body. The whale jerked wildly. This canoe had to move away quickly.

A second canoe came up from the other side. Another man thrust a harpoon into the whale. Long ropes and floats had been attached to the harpoons. The floats were seal skins filled with air. These made it hard for the animal to swim and dive. Now the whale was dragging two long ropes and many floats.

When the whale finally became tired, the canoes came in closer. The hunters killed the whale with more harpoons and pulled it to shore.

Everyone in the village came to meet the canoes as they paddled back to shore. The members of the Makah Tribe gave thanks for a safe hunt. Whale meat and oil were favorite foods. Everyone shared in the feast.

Today, hunting methods are very different, and so are the sources of food that we all have available to us. Many people think that since the American Indians of today have so many other resources for food, they shouldn't be allowed to hunt whales. Other people feel that it is important to keep the whale-hunting tradition going for the Makah. WHAT DO YOU THINK?

Before you make a decision, it's always a good idea to do some research. Share the story of the Makah Tribe. Ask people around you what their thoughts are on the topic and why they feel that way. Do some reading in books and even from trusted Internet sites. For example, here's a story you can access online: www.abcnews.go.com/US/story?id=90125. Remember to have an adult's permission whenever you're using the Internet!

Now, write a paragraph to share your opinion. Your first sentence should introduce your opinion. Do think the Makah Tribe should still be allowed to hunt whales? The following sentences (include at least three) should state the reasons why you've formed your opinion. Your last sentence can simply summarize your answer, restating your opinion to wrap things up!

THE GREAT MAKAH WORD HUNT

Hunting for WORDS is much safer than hunting for WHALES! Find 14 words from "The Great Debate" article that are hidden in the word search.

CANOES MAKAH	DEBATE OCEAN	FLOATS ROPES	FOOD SHORE	HARPOONS TRADITION	HUNT TRIBE	INDIANS WHALE

```
T  A  J  T  C  N  E  S  D  S  U  A  X  R  P
Y  R  N  P  S  M  D  N  E  T  T  I  J  S  Z
H  K  A  A  U  V  O  A  B  N  S  A  E  R  V
J  C  L  D  E  U  O  I  A  U  X  P  O  Q  Y
J  G  M  K  I  C  F  D  T  H  O  J  D  L  W
Z  O  A  D  S  T  O  N  E  R  G  K  S  S  F
J  C  K  U  F  Z  I  I  D  D  X  W  W  C  W
C  P  A  C  L  X  O  O  F  M  D  H  G  E  M
T  A  H  X  E  H  F  Y  N  D  A  J  L  I  W
P  N  N  R  D  C  M  U  D  R  M  J  I  G  A
M  B  X  O  P  E  X  X  P  W  E  R  O  H  S
G  M  N  U  E  R  G  O  D  H  E  B  I  R  T
M  H  N  K  M  S  O  C  C  A  X  S  K  G  L
I  F  A  W  F  N  G  G  G  L  X  A  N  W  Z
H  R  Z  I  S  P  A  K  Y  E  H  Q  R  V  O
```

A SNACK FOR A SAILOR

The next section of activities will have you "tweeting" away about early explorers to the Pacific Northwest. Before you get started, you might want some brain food! With the help of an adult, prepare this ship-shape snack.

INGREDIENTS

Gummy fish
An apple
2 sliced cheese squares (each about $1/4$ inch thick)
8 toothpicks
1 can lemon-lime soda
Blue food coloring

DIRECTIONS

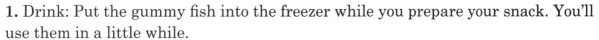

1. Drink: Put the gummy fish into the freezer while you prepare your snack. You'll use them in a little while.

2. Snack: Slice the apple into eight wedges.

3. Snack: Slice the cheese squares into 8 triangles.

4. Snack: Attach the cheese triangles to one end of each toothpick. Then poke the other end into each apple wedge. The apples are the boats, and the cheese slices make the sails. Do your snacks look like sailing ships?

5. Drink: Are you thirsty? How about some "seawater?" Pour a can of lemon-lime soda into a clear glass. Add 1 drop of blue food coloring and stir. Remove the gummy fish from the freezer and add a few to your drink.

EARLY EXPLORERS TO THE PACIFIC NORTHWEST: THE SPANISH

Indians had lived in the Pacific Northwest and the rest of the Americas for years and years, but it wasn't until the 1500s that non-Indian explorers began coming to the Pacific Northwest. These travelers wanted to learn about the new lands, and they hoped to find great riches. Ships from Spain, England, the United States (following the Revolutionary War), and other countries sailed along the coasts of North and South America exploring the unknown lands.

Read about some of the earliest explorers to the Pacific Northwest region.

Bartolome Ferrelo

The first explorer to see the Pacific Northwest from his ship was probably from Spain. Bartolome Ferrelo sailed up the Pacific Coast from Mexico. Like many of the early explorers, he did not find a safe place to land his ship, so he sailed away.

Juan de Fuca

It was another 50 years before Juan de Fuca headed up the Pacific Coast as captain of a Spanish ship. He told of a wide body of water that today is called the Strait of Juan de Fuca. However, he sailed on by and did not explore it.

Juan Perez

Over 180 years later, Juan Perez, another Spanish sailor, sailed north from today's Mexico. He tried to claim the land in the Pacific Northwest for Spain, but the weather was stormy, the coast was covered with fog, and his crew was sick. Instead, Perez and his crew stopped at a quiet cove called Nootka on today's Vancouver Island in Canada. Local Indians paddled out in canoes to Perez's ship and traded sea otter furs for beautiful shells. The Spanish had gathered the shells along the California coast. This might have been the beginning of the Spanish fur trade. The Indians traded animal skins for other items they wanted. After the short stop, Perez returned home.

Bruno de Heceta

The next year, Juan Perez again sailed up the coast. This time, he was on a ship under the command of Bruno de Heceta. Perez also took a second ship with its captain and crew. At a place that is now called Grenville Bay in Washington, some of the crew went ashore. They put a cross for the Catholic Church into the ground and buried a bottle. Inside the bottle was a piece of paper that had writing on it. The writing said the land now belonged to Spain. After only about an hour, the men returned by a small boat to the larger ship waiting out at sea. Then the captain of the second ship sent seven men to get fresh water and to cut firewood on the land. As their small boat went ashore, a large group of Indians came out of the forest and quickly killed all the men. Heceta watched in horror from his ship. Both ships sailed away as fast as they could.

Why Didn't Spain Settle the Northwest?

The Spanish claimed land along the coast, but they never settled there. Few Spanish explorers even went ashore. They were more interested in the fur trade. They built a fur-trading fort at Nootka and kept men there for many years.

SPANISH TWEETS

Can you imagine what it might have been like if these early explorers had taken smartphones with them on their journeys? Think of the information they could have shared with the whole world in just one tweet! What do you think these explorers would have posted in 140 characters or less? Have some fun imagining a conversation and creating the tweets that might have been exchanged!

@BFERRELO—EXPLORER "Nowhere safe to land a ship. Turned around. #explorerslife"

@CAPTAINDEFUCA

_____

_____

_____

@TRADING—JUANPEREZ

_____

_____

_____

@SADCAPTAINDEHECETA

_____

_____

_____

EARLY EXPLORERS TO THE PACIFIC NORTHWEST: THE ENGLISH

Read about another group of early explorers to the Pacific Northwest, the English.

Captain James Cook

Other countries did not like it when Spain started claiming land in the Pacific Northwest. Each country wanted to be the most powerful by claiming the most land.

Captain James Cook was an important English explorer. Before coming to the Northwest, he had already sailed around the world twice. On one of his trips, he found the sunny islands we now call Hawaii. He called them the Sandwich Islands.

When Cook later sailed by the Northwest, he kept his ships far offshore. However, he did stop for a short time in the harbor at Nootka. He saw, to his dismay, that the Spanish were already there, trading with the Indians for sea otter furs.

Feeling that his trip had been a failure, Cook sailed once again to the Sandwich Islands. Just as he was leaving one of the islands, he was killed by native people.

George Vancouver

An English sea captain, George Vancouver, also explored along the Northwest. Vancouver was no stranger to the region. He had already traveled to the Northwest on two other trips with Captain Cook.

This time, Vancouver left England with two ships and followed Cook's route. Vancouver was the first non-Indian to explore the many wonders of Puget Sound. He made the first maps of the region and claimed all the land around it for England. After stopping at Nootka for a short time, he sailed across the Pacific Ocean to spend the winter in the warm Sandwich Islands.

ENGLISH TWEETS

Can you imagine what it might have been like if these early explorers had taken smartphones with them on their journeys? Think of the information they could have shared with the whole world in just one tweet! What do you think these explorers would have posted in 140 characters or less? Have some fun imagining a conversation and creating the tweets that might have been exchanged!

@COOKAROUNDTHEWORLD

_____

_____

_____

@VANCOUVERWANTSANISLAND

_____

_____

_____

EARLY EXPLORERS TO THE PACIFIC NORTHWEST: THE AMERICANS

Read about another group of early explorers to the Pacific Northwest, the Americans.

Robert Gray

While explorers from Spain and England were sailing along the coast, a new country, the United States of America, lay on the other side of the continent.

George Washington was president of this new country. Washington and other Americans wanted Robert Gray to claim land in the Pacific Northwest for the United States. Gray was a trader. He loaded two ships with metal knives, beads, blankets, and other goods for trading with the Indians. With a crew of sailors, the ships sailed from Boston, Massachusetts, all the way around South America and up the Pacific Coast. After finally anchoring at Nootka, the men traded with Indians and filled the ships with sea otter furs.

A Trade Route to China and Back

A trade route is a route of travel over water or land that is used by traders. Gray left Nootka and sailed to China. There he traded the soft furs for Chinese silks, spices, and tea. The sights and sounds of China were a new adventure for Gray. When Gray left China, he sailed around Asia and Africa and across the Atlantic Ocean to Boston. He sold the Chinese goods in Boston at high prices.

Gray Enters the Columbia River

After only six weeks in Boston, Gray again sailed to the Pacific Northwest. He traded up and down the coast. One day, Gray saw what seemed to be a wide river. Could he sail into the river? His crew tried, but the water was very rough. Long sandbars blocked the way.

A month later, the men came back. They waited until the ocean tides were high enough to carry a boat over the sandbars. This time they made it! Gray sailed up the river and claimed all the land around it for the United States.

Indians took their canoes out to meet the explorers. Gray gave them nails and other metal objects in exchange for salmon, deer meat, and 450 sea otter pelts. A pelt is an animal skin with the fur still on it. After 10 days, Gray left and sailed to China again.

Gray was the first non-Indian to sail up the Columbia River. He was also the first American to sail around the world—twice. He started an important trade route to China. He also gave the United States a stronger claim to the Northwest.

AMERICAN TWEETS

Can you imagine what it might have been like if these early explorers had taken smartphones with them on their journeys? Think of the information they could have shared with the whole world in just one tweet! What do you think Robert Gray would have posted in 140 characters or less? Have some fun imagining creating the tweets that Robert Gray may have shared!

@IFOUNDTHECOLUMBIARIVER

_____

_____

_____

@IFOUNDTHECOLUMBIARIVER

_____

_____

_____

@IFOUNDTHECOLUMBIARIVER

_____

_____

_____

YOU'RE HIRED!

Pretend you are an executive with the Hudson's Bay Company, a fur-trading company headquartered at Fort Vancouver. You've been put in charge of training new trappers. The best way to do it is to include all of the most important information in a letter that goes to all the employees. Be sure to be very detailed!

Welcome to **Hudson's Bay Company**! You will love every minute you are trapping and trading for our company. Follow these directions to help you be a successful trapper.

Here are some supplies you will need to buy in order to survive in the wilderness:

_____   _____

_____   _____

_____   _____

Your job will be to trap

_____

The furs you trap will be sold to

_____

and used for

_____

Trapping can be a dangerous job because . . .

_____

Trapping and trading is an important business because . . .

_____

The best part of working for our company is . . .

_____

THE FUR TRADE MAZE

Being a fur trader was hard work. The trader had to gather furs and pelts from all over the place to make a living. Help this trader get to the trading post with his furs.

LEWIS AND CLARK LIMERICK

Limericks are fun poems that have five lines. Lines 1, 2, and 5 rhyme and are long lines. Lines 3 and 4 rhyme and are short lines. Write a limerick about the Lewis and Clark Expedition.

Here is an example:
There was an explorer named Clark,
On a journey he said he'd embark.
He explored a great land,
Lewis gave him a hand,
And on history Clark left his mark.

1. _____

_____

_____

2. _____

_____

_____

3. _____

_____

4. _____

_____

5. _____

_____

"WHEEL" YOU PLEASE DRAW SOME PICTURES?

Once you've finished your Lewis and Clark limerick, illustrate it like a comic strip. Write each line in its box and then draw a cartoon below.

1
_____

2
_____

3
_____

4
_____

5
_____

A DAY IN THE LIFE OF AN EXPLORER

Imagine that you were a member of the Lewis and Clark Expedition back in 1805. You have been traveling west for almost a year and a half. Some of the members of the expedition have never seen the Pacific Ocean. When your group finally reaches the Pacific Ocean,

_____

_____

_____

_____

_____

_____

_____

_____

_____

_____

_____

what might you be thinking, feeling, seeing, or hearing as you saw it for the first time? Write a journal entry from the point of view of a member of the expedition.

_____

_____

_____

_____

_____

_____

_____

_____

_____

_____

_____

WHAT CAN YOU SEE IN THE SEA?

Have you ever been to the coast? What about the beach of a lake or the bank of a river? Washington has all three!

With two paper plates and some simple art supplies, you can make a fun project to illustrate what you can see in the sea!

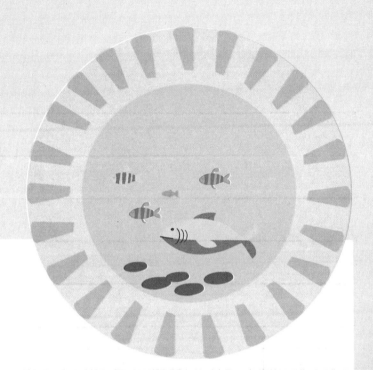

YOU WILL NEED:

2 paper plates
Glue
Scissors
Crayons or markers
Colored paper
Blue paint
Craft supplies to represent things you'd see in the ocean

DIRECTIONS:

1. Paint both paper plates blue. Once the paint has dried, cut the center out of one of the plates.
2. Decorate the uncut plate to represent an ocean scene. Be creative!
3. Glue the cut plate upside-down on top of the uncut plate to make a picture frame.

John C. Fremont led multiple expeditions all over what is now the western United States. The reports he brought back about the land made many people eager to move west. Fremont's wife, Jessie Benton Fremont, said to her husband, "All your campfires have become cities."

What do you think she meant by this statement?

_____

_____

_____

_____

_____

Who might have liked and disliked the changes Fremont's wife was referring to? Why?

_____

_____

_____

_____

_____

SETTLERS AND INDIANS

As more and more settlers came to Washington, Indians began to be pushed off their lands. Some settlers and Indians were able to live peacefully together. Other times, Indians and settlers fought with one another over the land. In the end, most Indians were forced into signing agreements with the U.S. government that they would give up their land in exchange for small pieces of land set aside for the Indians. These were called reservations.

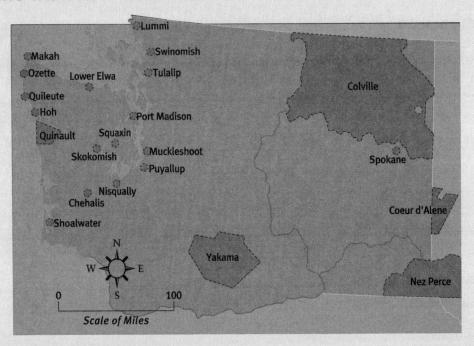

Imagine you are an Indian leader. You are faced with a difficult decision. If you keep fighting, more of your people will die. If you agree to peace, you will be moved to a reservation. The reservation is not as good for your people as the land you are fighting for. What would you do?

FIELD TRIP: NATIVE AMERICAN HERITAGE

Washington State is rich with Native American heritage and culture. If you want to learn more about Washington's Indian Tribes, there are many exhibits to visit throughout the state.

With the help of an adult, do some online research to find a museum, interpretive center, or state park near you. Plan a field trip with your family!

Now, pretend like you are a leader in a Native American tribe. Write a letter to your children and grandchildren, explaining to them why it's important to preserve your tribe's culture for future generations.

SCIENCE

188 Weather Wizards

189 Kids Can Forecast, Too!

190 Cloud Your Vision

192 Cloud Gazing

193 Cloudy, with a Chance of Rainbows

194 A Climo-what?

196 Wonderful Water

198 The Water Cycle

200 Climate Experiment

202 Hydroelectricity

203 Field Trip: Grand Coulee Dam

204 Inside a Volcano

205 Make a Volcano at Home

206 The Rock Cycle

210 Rock Hunt

211 Edible Igneous Rocks

212 Edible Sedimentary Rocks

213 Edible Metamorphic Rocks

214 From Weathered Rocks to Soils

215 Field Trip: Bellevue Botanical Garden

216 What's in Your Soil?

218 Soil Never Tasted So Good!

219 Worm Maze

220 It's in the Dirt Word Search

221 Hands on Field Trip

222 What Once Roamed the Earth

225 Field Trip: Stonerose Interpretive Center

226 Minerals at Home

WEATHER WIZARDS

Washington's weather can vary greatly across the state. It might be cool and rainy on one side of the state and hot and dry on the other side, all in the same day. Record the weather patterns of your city over a ten-day period. Do the same for a Washington city far from where you live. Compare your findings to learn just how crazy Washington's weather can be! Visit a local website like www.wsdot.com/traffic/weather or a national weather website, such as www.weather.com to find the information for the faraway city.

	YOUR CITY HIGH TEMPERATURE	YOUR CITY PRECIPITATION	COMPARISON CITY HIGH TEMPERATURE	COMPARISON CITY PRECIPITATION
Day 1				
Day 2				
Day 3				
Day 4				
Day 5				
Day 6				
Day 7				
Day 8				
Day 9				
Day 10				

Describe how your weather compares to that of the faraway city.

_____

_____

Why do you think your weather findings were similar/different?

_____

_____

Which city's weather do you prefer? Why?

_____

_____

KIDS CAN FORECAST, TOO!

Check out this video of a 10-year-old student doing a weather forecast on Halloween Day in Chicago, IL. Make sure you have an adult's permission before you go online.

www.youtube.com/watch?v=14n7kPW67HE

Now pretend you are a weather forecaster. What would you like most about giving a weather report?

_____

_____

_____

What do you think would be most difficult?

_____

_____

Draw a picture of yourself giving the weather report.

CLOUD YOUR VISION

The clouds can tell us a lot about the weather. There are three main types of clouds: stratus, cumulus, and cirrus. Read about the different types below. Then use the information to help Megan and Dan decide what to wear to school.

Stratus Clouds

Stratus clouds are the clouds closest to the ground and seem to blanket the sky. At about 6,500 feet, they can produce rain, drizzle, snow, or mist.

Cumulus Clouds

Cumulus clouds are puffy and white. Often they are flat on the bottom and rise up in the sky like huge pieces of cotton. They form up to 20,000 feet above the ground. Cumulus clouds usually mean fair weather, but they sometimes grow very large and become thunderheads. As these clouds gather, they create thunder and lightning and produce rain and hail.

Cirrus Clouds

Cirrus clouds are thin, curly, wispy clouds. They form 25,000 to 40,000 feet above the ground. They are so high that the water droplets freeze into ice crystals. Cirrus clouds generally signal an incoming storm or a change in weather.

What kind of clouds Megan and Dan saw out the window this morning:	What you think the weather might be like today:	What kinds of clothes and shoes you think Megan and Dan should wear to school today:
GREY STRATUS CLOUDS BLANKET THE SKY.		
EVEN MORE AND DARKER STRATUS CLOUDS BLANKET THE SKY.		
THE SUN IS SHINING AND THERE ARE A FEW CIRRUS CLOUDS IN THE SKY.		
THE SUN IS SHINING AND WHITE CUMULUS CLOUDS ARE IN THE SKY.		
VERY LARGE GREY CUMULUS CLOUDS ARE IN THE SKY.		

CLOUD GAZING

Sometimes people see shapes in the clouds like animals or faces. Spend 30 minutes or more just lying on a blanket in the grass looking at the sky. Did you see any fun shapes in the clouds while you were gazing? Draw a picture of what you saw.

CLOUDY, WITH A CHANCE OF RAINBOWS

Not a cloud in the sky? That's okay! Make one indoors. The good news is that this one won't rain on you!

YOU WILL NEED:

White poster paper
Scissors
Paper streamers/crepe paper (red, orange, yellow, green, blue, and purple)
Markers or crayons
Cotton balls
Glue

DIRECTIONS:

1. Draw a cloud on the poster paper and cut it out.
2. Glue streamers on the back of the cloud in the order of the colors in the rainbow.
3. Draw and color a friendly face on the front of the cloud.
4. Stretch out cotton balls and glue them all around the cloud. Be sure not to cover up the face.

A climograph is a graph that shows the average temperatures and precipitation of a place. This climograph shows data for Seattle, Washington's capital city. Study the graph and answer the questions.

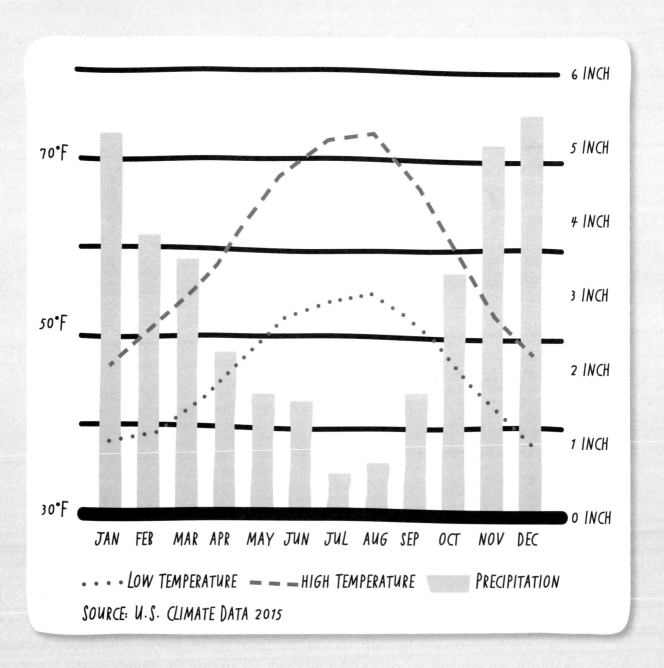

···· LOW TEMPERATURE — — — HIGH TEMPERATURE ▢ PRECIPITATION

SOURCE: U.S. CLIMATE DATA 2015

1. Which color line represents the average high temperatures?

_____

2. Which color line represents the average low temperatures?

_____

3. Each line represents an increase of how many degrees?

_____

4. How are the amounts of precipitation represented?

_____

5. During which month(s) does Seattle reach its highest temperatures?

_____

6. During which month(s) does Seattle reach its lowest temperatures?

_____

7. Describe the pattern the high temperatures follow through the year.

_____

_____

8. Describe the pattern the low temperatures follow through the year.

_____

_____

9. Describe the pattern the precipitation follows through the year.

_____

_____

10. Do you think there is a relationship between the temperatures and the precipitation levels? Defend your answer with data from the climograph.

_____

_____

_____

WONDERFUL WATER

Many of Washington's coastal cities are known for their rainfall. Water is an important natural resource here!

Why do coastal areas get so much more rain than the areas inland? Understanding the water cycle will help you answer that question!

Read about the water cycle and label each step of the cycle on the diagram.

EVAPORATION: It all starts with heat from the sun. As the sun heats water, the water evaporates. That means it turns into vapor, or steam. The vapor rises into the air. Have you ever noticed a puddle that was there one day and gone the next? Where did the water go? It evaporated. Can you see the word vapor in evaporate? The ocean provides an endless supply of water for the sun to evaporate.

CONDENSATION: When the water vapor in the air gets cold, it condenses (gets thicker) and turns back into liquid. You have seen this happen when you pour a glass of cold water on a hot day. Drops of water form on the outside of the glass. It also happens to the cool mirror in the bathroom when you take a hot shower. As water condenses, clouds form. As more water condenses, the clouds get heavier.

PRECIPITATION: Pretty soon the air can no longer hold all that water. The water falls to the ground as rain, hail, sleet, or snow. This is called precipitation. The type of precipitation is based on the temperature.

COLLECTION: The falling water collects where it lands. It may fall in the rivers, lakes, and oceans. It may sink into the earth and become groundwater. Water that flows off the surface is called runoff. In time, it flows into the ocean or lakes. Then the cycle starts all over again.

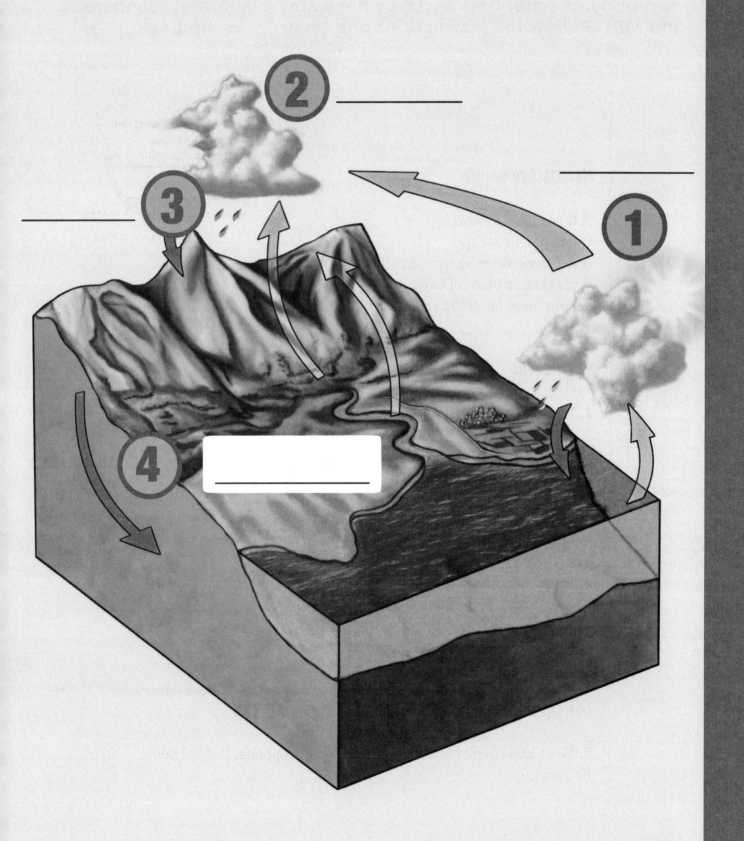

THE WATER CYCLE

Do you want to see the water cycle in action? You can create your own body of water and watch as the water evaporates, condenses, and falls. Follow the instructions and record your findings.

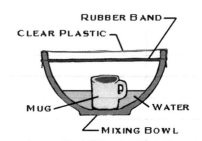

MATERIALS TO GATHER:

A large plastic bowl
Clear plastic wrap
A dry ceramic mug (like a coffee mug)
A marker or piece of tape
A long piece of string or large rubber band
Water

INSTRUCTIONS:

1. Put the large bowl outside in a sunny place.

2. Put the mug inside the bowl.

3. Add water into the bowl around the mug until it reaches up about $^2/_3$ the height of the mug. Be careful not to get any water inside the mug.

4. If you can, mark the beginning water level on the outside of the bowl with a marker or a piece of tape.

5. Cover the top of the bowl tightly with plastic wrap.

6. Either tie the string around the bowl or use the rubber band to help keep the plastic wrap on tight.

7. Wait and check back often to see what happens. Record your findings.

TIME Record the time you look at the bowl.	FINDINGS Record what you see.	CONCLUSIONS Record why you think things look like they do at this time.
START TIME:		
30 MINUTES LATER:		
ONE HOUR LATER:		
TWO HOURS LATER:		
THREE HOURS LATER:		
THE FOLLOWING DAY:		

CLIMATE EXPERIMENT

Do you think water or soil holds heat longer? Knowing the answer to this question can help you understand why the climate near the ocean and the climate farther away from the ocean are so different.

1. Gather two empty soup cans.

2. Fill one with room temperature water and the other with soil.

3. Place a thermometer in each can.

4. Record the temperatures of each can.

5. Place both cans under a lamp or on a windowsill in direct sunlight.

6. Record the temperatures of each can every three minutes. Do this for 15 minutes.

7. Remove the cans from the light or sunlight and continue to record the temperatures every three minutes for 15 minutes.

8. What conclusions can you draw? Which holds heat longer, soil or water?

_____

_____

9. How might this experiment help you understand the climate of locations near the ocean and the climate of locations far from the ocean?

_____

_____

	CAN WITH WATER	CAN WITH SOIL
Beginning temperature		
Temperature after 3 minutes in the light		
Temperature after 6 minutes in the light		
Temperature after 9 minutes in the light		
Temperature after 12 minutes in the light		
Temperature after 15 minutes in the light		
Temperature after 3 minutes out of the light		
Temperature after 6 minutes out of the light		
Temperature after 9 minutes out of the light		
Temperature after 12 minutes out of the light		
Temperature after 15 minutes out of the light		

HYDROELECTRICITY

According to the U.S. Energy Information Administration, Washington's number one energy source is hydroelectricity (Source: www.eia.gov/state/?sid=WA). Hydropower is electricity created from the energy of moving water. Dams are built across many of Washington's rivers. The moving water turns the blades of turbines, which produces electricity.

Many people are in favor of hydroelectricity because it is a source of power that will not run out. It is also considered a clean source of energy because it does not leave behind waste. However, the ecosystems of many rivers have been interrupted to build dams, create reservoirs, and harness the energy.

You can learn more about hydroelectricity online at www.eia.gov/kids/energy.cfm?page=hydropower_home-basics. Remember to let an adult know before you use the Internet.

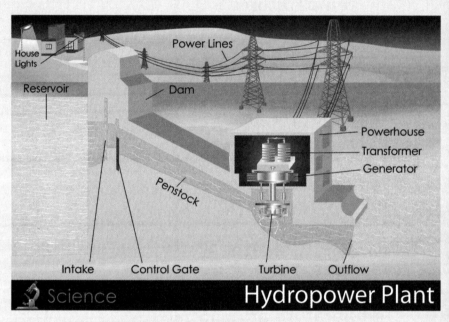

Hydropower Plant

What do you think? Should additional dams be built to rely more on hydroelectricity? Or should the ecosystems in and near the rivers be left alone? Share your opinion, giving at least three reasons to support it.

_____

_____

_____

_____

FIELD TRIP: GRAND COULEE DAM

The Grand Coulee Dam on the Columbia River is the largest producer of hydroelectric power in the United States. You can learn more about visiting the Grand Coulee Dam at www.gcdvisitor.com. Plan a field trip with your family!

Although the Grand Coulee Dam is the largest, there are many other hydroelectric dams in Washington State. See the below website for a list.

www.visiteverycityinwashingtonstate.com/MiscPages/dams/dammainpage.htm

*Remember to have an adult's permission before you go online.

What kind of things did you see at the dam?

_____

_____

_____

_____

_____

_____

_____

_____

What was the most interesting thing you saw?

_____

_____

_____

Why?

_____

_____

_____

_____

INSIDE A VOLCANO

One of Washington's most famous landmarks is Mt. Saint Helens. This active volcano last erupted on July 10, 2008. However, its most famous large eruption was in 1980, when the north face of the mountain collapsed and magma flattened vegetation and buildings over a distance of 230 square miles. For more than nine hours, ash spewed from the volcano, eventually reaching 12 to 16 miles above sea level.

This image shows a cross-section of a volcano. Can you label all the parts of a volcano? Use the terms in the word bank to label each part.

ASH	ASH CLOUD	BRANCH PIPE	FLANK	LAVA FLOW	LAYERS
MAGMA CHAMBER	PIPE	ROCK LAYERS	SIDE VENT	SILL	VENT

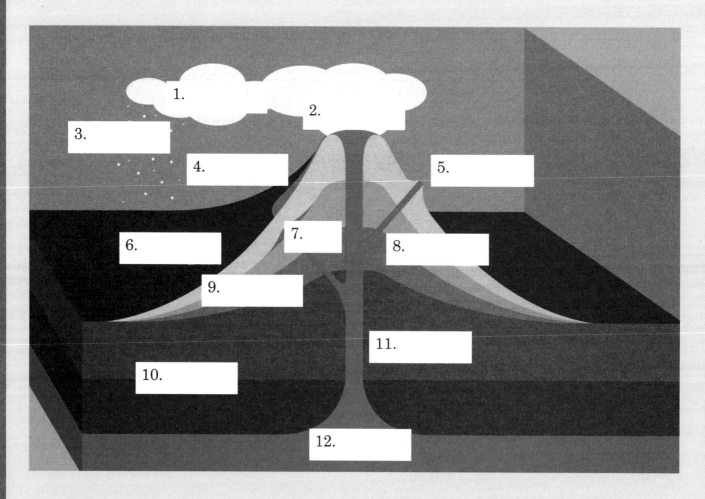

MAKE A VOLCANO AT HOME

You've probably seen how the reaction between baking soda and vinegar creates a chemical volcano. Many kids your age make volcanoes like this for science projects at home or at school.

There are also other fun ways to make a volcano. You can use yeast and hydrogen peroxide, ketchup and baking soda, diet soda and Mentos candies, and even dry ice!

With the permission of an adult, visit this website to choose which type of volcano you'd like to make: www.sciencenotes.org/5-ways-to-make-a-volcano.

When you make your volcano, have a camera handy so you can take a picture of it! Print your photo and paste it on this page.

Which type of chemical volcano did you choose to make?

_____

Did it work well? Why or why not?

_____

_____

_____

THE ROCK CYCLE

Washington State has at least 63 named mountain ranges. The mountains are made up of different kinds of rock, depending on how the mountains were formed.

Every rock belongs to one of three rock groups: sedimentary, igneous, or metamorphic. Rocks belong to a rock group based on how the rock was formed. Over millions of years, rocks become each type of rock, changing as heat and pressure are applied to them.

Sedimentary: Rocks are broken down into small particles called sediment. The rocks are broken down by sun, wind, and water over long periods of time. The sediments collect in layers. Over time, these layers build up. Sometimes, the minerals in the sediment dissolve in the water. They create a "cement" that binds the layers together. As this happens, a solid rock is formed.

Conglomerate is "nature's concrete." It develops when floods or landslides create gravel and sand deposits.
Sandstone is made up of medium-size sand grains cemented together. Siltstone is made of finer grain sand.
Shale is formed when the water is squeezed out of layers of mud.
Limestone is made of the shells of tiny sea animals.

There are four main types of sedimentary rock in Washington.

Igneous: Igneous rocks form when melted rock (called magma) rises from inside the earth and cools. If the magma cools beneath the surface, the cooling takes many years. The igneous rocks that form beneath the surface may have crystals in them.

If the magma cools on the surface, it cools more quickly. The rocks formed may have bubbles or be very smooth, like glass.

Igneous rocks are "fire formed." In Washington, **basalt** is fine-grained, dark lava rock. **Granite** forms when the earth cools underneath volcanoes. **Rhyolite** is created by ash deposits, erupted from volcanoes like Mt. Saint Helens. **Andesite** is formed by layers of lava and ash, from the eruption of volcanoes like Mt. Rainier.

Metamorphic: Metamorphic rocks have been changed inside the earth by extreme heat and pressure. These rocks may contain crystals. Sometimes the crystals are called gems because of their value. Rubies, sapphires, and garnets are found in metamorphic rocks.

Some of the metamorphic rocks in Washington include **argillite**, **slate**, **phyllite**, **schist**, **gneiss**, **marble**, **quartzite**, **greenstone**, **fault breccia**, and **mylonite**. These rocks form when other types of rock have been "squeezed and cooked" and become recrystallized.

Draw a picture of each kind of rock in the rock cycle. Then decide which type of rock is described in the questions.

IGNEOUS

METAMORPHIC

SEDIMENTARY

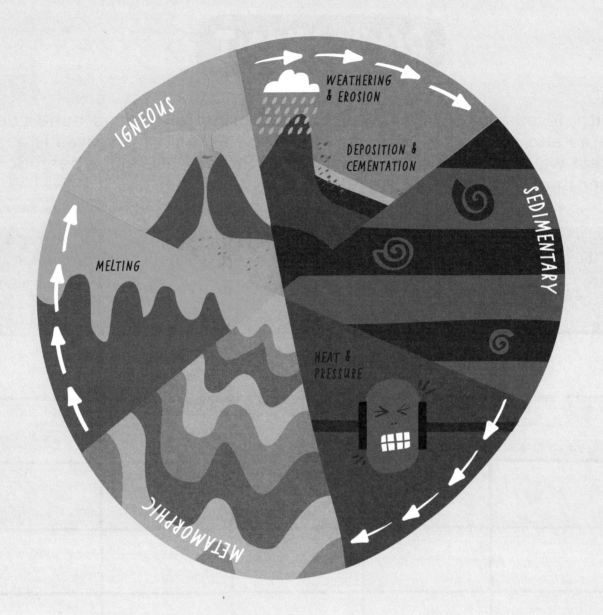

1. There was activity inside an active volcano. No magma ever made it outside of the volcano. The magma inside the volcano cooled over many years and turned into rock.

_____

2. A rocky mountain peak is beat with wind and rain over many years. The rock is broken down and the sediment gathers below the peak, where it is "cemented" together.

_____

3. At a fault line, sedimentary rock is pushed beneath the earth's surface. Over many years, heat and pressure are applied to the rock.

_____

ROCK HUNT

With permission from an adult, go exploring for rocks around your home and collect six of them. Studying the rocks in an area is a great way to learn what kind of work Mother Nature has been doing over many, many years! Record your findings below.

Draw a picture of the rock.	Does the rock have layers or many small pieces cemented together?	Is the rock shiny or dull?	Does the rock have crystals?	Is the rock made of heavy or light material?
1.				
2.				
3.				
4.				
5.				
6.				

Choose three rocks. Use the details of the rock to draw a conclusion about which group of rocks it may belong to, igneous, sedimentary, or metamorphic.

Rock _____ is probably a _____ rock because _____

Rock _____ is probably a _____ rock because _____

Rock _____ is probably a _____ rock because _____

EDIBLE IGNEOUS ROCKS

Have an adult help you make your own igneous rocks.

WHAT YOU WILL NEED:

1 bag white chocolate chips
1 bag milk or semisweet chocolate chips
Waxed paper
A cookie sheet
A stirring spoon
A saucepan with a double boiler

INSTRUCTIONS:

1. Fill the saucepan with water and place it on the stove. Turn on the burner and place the double boiler on top of the saucepan.

2. Place the different rock types (white and chocolate chips) in the double boiler.

3. Stir the rocks until the heat begins to combine the different rock types into hot magma.

4. Line the cookie sheet with wax paper.

5. Pour the hot magma onto the wax paper to cool, just like magma cools on the earth's surface.

6. When the chocolate magma has finished cooling, break it into pieces and enjoy your new, tasty igneous rocks!

EDIBLE SEDIMENTARY ROCKS

Have an adult help you make your own sedimentary rocks.

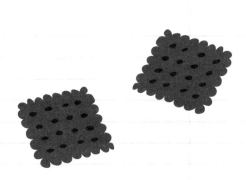

WHAT YOU WILL NEED:

Graham crackers
Frosting
Utensils to spread frosting

INSTRUCTIONS:

1. On a plate, place the first layer of rock sediment, a graham cracker.

2. Put some frosting on the cracker to represent the minerals that have dissolved and created cement.

3. Place another layer of rock sediment on next, a graham cracker.

4. Continue layering rocks and "cement," as many as you would like.

5. Enjoy your tasty sedimentary rock!

EDIBLE METAMORPHIC ROCKS

Have an adult help you make your own metamorphic rocks.

WHAT YOU WILL NEED:

Sugar cookie dough (dyed in three colors)
A cookie sheet
Oven or toaster oven

INSTRUCTIONS:

1. Take a small piece of each kind of rock, the different colors of cookie dough.

2. Combine all three kinds of rocks and apply pressure by smashing them all together.

3. You can even fold the dough and apply more pressure.

4. Apply heat to the rocks by baking the cookies in the oven. Follow baking directions for the sugar cookie recipe you used.

5. Once the rocks have cooled down, break one in half to see the different layers that created the metamorphic rock.

6. Enjoy your tasty metamorphic rock!

FROM WEATHERED ROCKS TO SOILS

When rocks are weathered and when plants die, their broken-down remains create soil. The soil profile is what you would see if you could cut a slice out of the earth's surface. Study the soil profile and answer the questions.

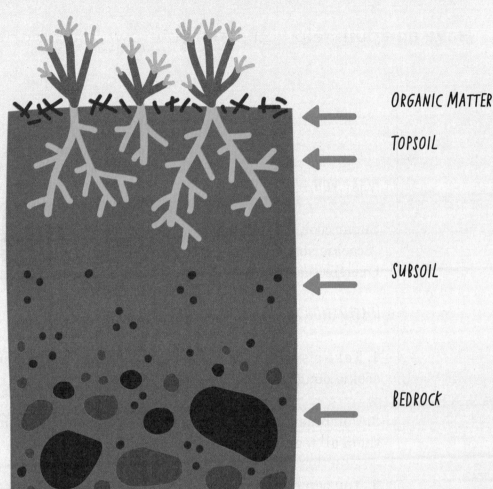

ORGANIC MATTER

TOPSOIL

SUBSOIL

BEDROCK

1. In which layer of the soil do plants grow?

_____

2. Where are the largest rocks and materials? Why do you think they are there?

_____

_____

3. Where are the darkest materials? Why do you think they are there?

_____

_____

FIELD TRIP: BELLEVUE BOTANICAL GARDEN

The Bellevue Botanical Garden is a 53-acre nature center in King County where visitors can explore gardens, woodlands, and wetlands. You can learn more about this beautiful place at www.bellevuebotanical.org.

Ask an adult to help you plan a garden getaway for your family! If Bellevue is too far to travel, here is a wiki-list of additional options in Washington: www.en.wikipedia.org/wiki/List_of_botanical_gardens_and_arboretums_in_Washington_.

Where are you going to go? _____

Take a notebook with you to the garden you visit and record the following information.

Write down the names of three plant species you've seen before.

_____

_____

_____

Write down the names of three plant species you've never seen before.

_____

_____

_____

Observe the soil type(s) you see in the garden. Describe any differences you notice among soil types.

_____

Ask an employee why the garden you visit is important to the community. Record his or her answer.

_____

_____

_____

WHAT'S IN YOUR SOIL?

Have you wondered what is in the soil around your house? Try this experiment to learn more about the soil near you.

WHAT YOU WILL NEED:

A glass jar with a lid
Water
Small shovel

INSTRUCTIONS:

1. Use a small shovel to get about a cup of soil from around your house.

2. First, make sure to remove any surface debris, and then dig a few inches down.

3. Put the soil in the jar.

4. Fill the jar about three-quarters full with water.

5. Put the lid on tight and shake the jar for about one minute.

6. Set down the jar and let it sit still.

7. Record your findings.

Record what you see after one minute:

_____

Record what you see after two minutes:

_____

Record what you see after five minutes:

_____

Record what you see after ten minutes:

_____

Record what you see after one day:

_____

Draw a picture of your soil jar. Label the different layers.

Measure the bottom layer (sand): _____

Measure the second layer (silt): _____

Measure the top layer (clay): _____

Do you have any items still floating around in the top of the water? If so, record what you see. The floating items are organic matter, parts of dead plants and animals that become part of the soil over time.

_____

_____

_____

How would you describe your soil overall?

_____

_____

SOIL NEVER TASTED SO GOOD!

With the help of an adult, make soil profile treats for your family!

WHAT YOU WILL NEED:

Shredded coconut, slivered almonds, and gummy worms (organic matter)
Finely crushed chocolate cookies (topsoil)
Chocolate pudding (subsoil)
Candy-coated chocolate pieces (bedrock)
Clear plastic cups
Permanent marker

INSTRUCTIONS:

1. Put a layer of candy-coated chocolate pieces in the bottom of each cup.

2. Next put a layer of chocolate pudding in each cup.

3. Then put a layer crushed chocolate cookies in each cup.

4. Put a final layer of shredded coconut, slivered almonds, and gummy worms in each cup.

5. With a permanent marker, label each layer on the outside of the cups.

WORM MAZE

This poor worm is lost in the grass. Help Werner Worm find his way back to his home.

IT'S IN THE DIRT WORD SEARCH

Now that you know all about rocks and soil, find the missing words in the below puzzle by circling them.

SEDIMENTARY   IGNEOUS   METAMORPHIC   ORGANIC MATTER

TOPSOIL   SUBSOIL   BEDROCK   SOIL

```
S V H S X R N S Q B C B O G L I G W N O
J O T Q E B N B G I Y R Z T F G U O K V
P M W O I D Z Y H W Q H Q W Q O E O C D
X B R C P Z I P X A V S Z S L Z E K P G
V N M F A S R N S Y G G Q R O W C F E
I H H X V O O I E I A Y W E N M N T P H
I G B V M F C I Y N B J I Q F N H R S M
C H N A V M J C L Y T L J B N T L R C R
A L T E A V U X G B F A S Z R F G R V N
L E T T O K B W Y K I J R P D G M D J I
M B T D I U T G O H M P S Y B J X P P R
O E F J P B S A B J N J U Z Y Z T Y A D
R O B J K B V M F P P H B M Y G I J E Z
D B J M N O L L K W R K S V T X J I O W
Q B E X L I C P A Q D R O L M Q J P A D
P B P D Y R O I K A S E I V I T N F W P
T R G I R A O Q N V I A L H S O B X Q A
P J N Q Z O O W C N L D Y M Q R S D M T
A F D T P Z C N S O C N R V Q W B U U S
W O B L O F L K Q X P H J G A T T Y T G
```

HANDS ON FIELD TRIP

The Hands On Children's Museum in Olympia is a great place for kids to learn about science and art. The museum welcomes more than 300,000 visitors each year. With the help of an adult, learn more about this organization at www.hocm.org, and plan a field trip with your family.

What was your favorite exhibit?

_____

_____

Why?

_____

_____

_____

How would you describe the Hands on Children's Museum to someone who has never been there before?

_____

_____

_____

_____

_____

_____

WHAT ONCE ROAMED THE EARTH

Many animals that once roamed the land in Washington are now extinct. They no longer live anywhere on earth. How could we possibly know about creatures that lived millions of years ago? Some of the most important clues are fossils. A fossil is a mark or the remains of an ancient plant or animal. There are different types of fossils, and they are named based on how they are formed.

Impressions show the outline of a living thing. Impressions are created when thin plants and small animals die in sediment. As they rot, they leave behind a dark print of the organism. Plants, leaves, feathers, and fish often become impressions.

Make your own impression fossils with clay or dough. Using small household items, press them into clay and have others guess what you used to make each impression.

Molds and casts are impressions made by larger organisms. When an organism dies and is covered with sediment, its body slowly breaks down. A hole, or mold, is left in its place. If the hole is filled with sediment, it produces a cast. The cast looks like the original organism on the outside.

Make your own mold and cast fossil with plaster from a craft store. Put some wet plaster in

a cup. Place a small item in the plaster, covering the top of it with the plaster. Let the plaster dry overnight. The next day, carefully chisel the plaster in half and remove the item you left in the plaster. Fill the empty mold with clay to take on the shape of the mold. Remove the clay and have others guess what the item was.

Traces are impressions that show traces of activity. These include footprints, teeth marks, tracks, and tail prints. How does a trace become a fossil? An impression must be left in soft sediment. As the sediment hardens, the track is preserved (kept the same) after being quickly covered with more sediment.

You can make your own trace fossils with leaves, paper, and crayons. Put a piece of paper over a leaf and rub the paper with the side of a peeled crayon. The crayon rubbing should reveal the shape of the leaf on the paper.

Mineral replacements form from hard body parts, such as bones, teeth, claws, or shells. These are also called petrified fossils. Over time, more and more sediment buries the remains. The bone slowly dissolves. Water filled with minerals seeps in. It replaces the bone with a rock-like material. The fossil has the same shape and size as the object, but the color of the minerals. It is harder and heavier than the original.

You can make your own mineral replacement fossils with ice cube trays. If you can, use trays that make ice cubes shaped like different objects. When you fill the tray with water, it represents the water that seeps into the body part and dissolves it, leaving behind a harder and heavier material in the shape of the object.

Amber can preserve an organism whole. For example, an insect might have been trapped in tree sap. The sap slowly turns into amber, and the organism is preserved. Entire animals have also been preserved by being frozen or stuck in sticky tar pits.

You can make your own amber fossils with the help of an adult, who will use a hot glue gun. Place a small item, such as a penny, on a piece of paper. Ask an adult to cover the item with hot glue. The glue represents the amber that preserves the organism whole. After the glue cools, examine your amber fossil.

FIELD TRIP: STONEROSE INTERPRETIVE CENTER

Did you know that you can go hunt for fossils of your own at the Stonerose Interpretive Center & Eocene Fossil Site? This cool place is located in the town of Republic.

With the help of an adult, visit www.stonerosefossil.org to plan a trip to visit 48 million year-old fossil beds.

Did you find a fossil?

_____

What did you find?

_____

List three things you learned on your field trip.

_____

_____

_____

Draw a picture of what you found.

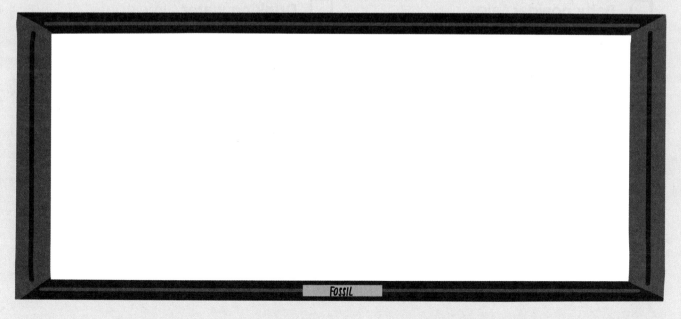

FOSSIL

MINERALS AT HOME

Washington is a land of many valuable rocks and minerals. Study this list of some of the common minerals found in a home. Put a check by any of the minerals that you have in your home.

- ☐ **Carpet** Calcium carbonate, limestone

- ☐ **Glass/Ceramics** Silica sand, limestone, talc, lithium, borates, soda ash, feldspar

- ☐ **Cake/Bread** Gypsum, phosphates

- ☐ **Plant fertilizers** Potash, phosphate, nitrogen, sulfur

- ☐ **Toothpaste** Calcium carbonate, limestone, sodium carbonate, fluorine

- ☐ **Lipstick** Calcium carbonate, talc

- ☐ **Baby powder** Talc

- ☐ **Household cleaners** Silica, pumice, diatomite, feldspar, limestone

- ☐ **Jewelry** Precious and semi-precious stones

- ☐ **Kitty litter** Attapulgite, montmorillonite, zeolites, diatomite, pumice, volcanic ash

- ☐ **Potting soil** Vermiculite, perlite, gypsum, zeolites, peat

- ☐ **Paint** Titanium dioxide, kaolin clays, calcium carbonate, mica, talc, silica, wollastonite

- ☐ **Microwavable container** Talc, calcium carbonate, titanium dioxide, clay

- ☐ **Sports equipment** Graphite, fiberglass

- ☐ **Pots and pans** Aluminum, iron

- ☐ **Fruit juice** Perlite, diatomite

- ☐ **Sugar** Limestone, lime

- ☐ **Drinking water** Limestone, lime, salt, fluorite

- ☐ **Television** 35 different minerals

- ☐ **Automobile** 15 different minerals

- ☐ **Telephone** 42 different minerals

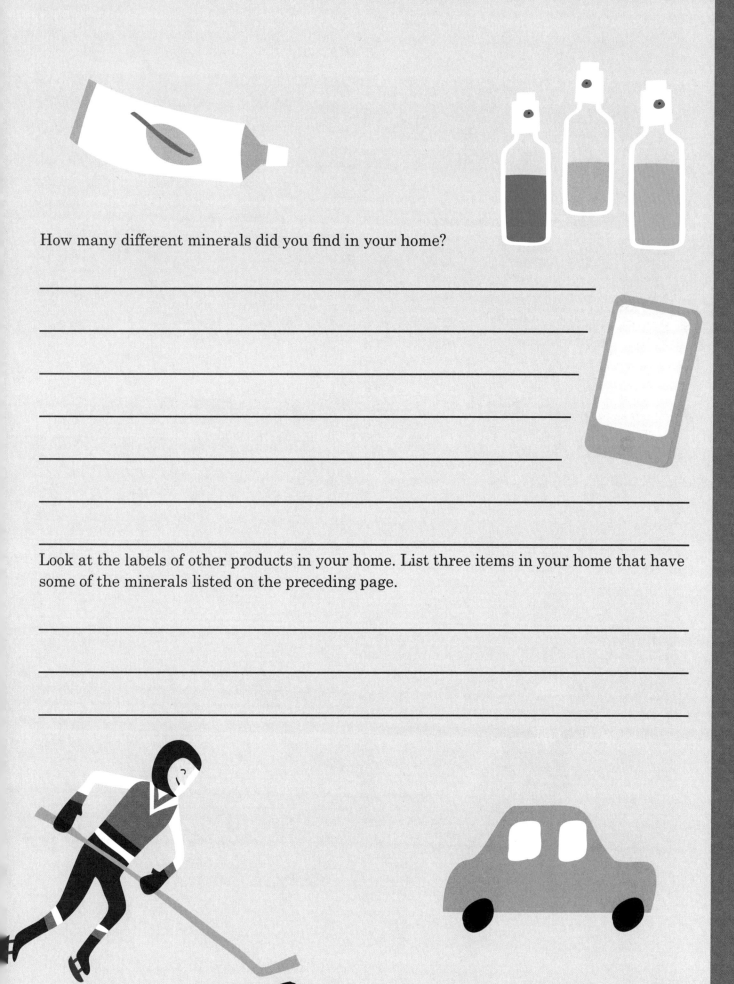

How many different minerals did you find in your home?

_____

_____

_____

_____

_____

_____

Look at the labels of other products in your home. List three items in your home that have some of the minerals listed on the preceding page.

_____

_____

_____

MATH

230 The Largest Grid in the World

231 Washington's Latitude and Longitude

232 Elevation Exploration

235 Field Trip: Take a Hike!

236 Create a Map of Your Bedroom

238 Let's "Sea" Some Salaries!

240 Field Trip: Seahawks Game

241 Compute the Commute

242 Sounders' Goals

243 Mariners Baseball

244 The First People

245 How Far Is a Mile?

246 Understand Dates and Timelines

247 Math for the Journey West

248 Along the Nez Perce Trail

249 Railroads Bring Change

250 Brain Teaser

251 Employment in Washington

252 Washington's Top 10 Exports

253 Washington's Top 10 Trading Partners for Exports

THE LARGEST GRID IN THE WORLD

You can use latitude and longitude to find a location anywhere on Earth.

LATITUDE LINES
Run side to side
Measure °North and °South of the equator

LONGITUDE LINES
Run up and down
Measure °East and °West of the prime meridian

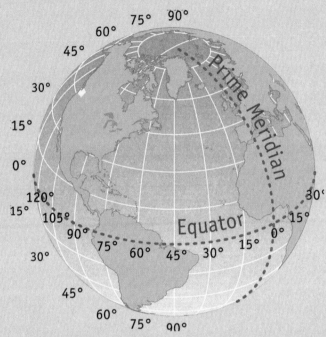

1. Washington is located above which line of latitude?

_____

2. Which two continents straddle the equator?

_____

3. Which two continents straddle the prime meridian?

_____

4. Which continent is clearly located in the northern hemisphere?

_____

5. In which hemisphere is the north pole located?

_____

6. In which hemisphere is the south pole located?

_____

7. Is Washington found in the northern or southern hemisphere?

_____

8. Is Washington found in the eastern or western hemisphere?

_____

9. How would you describe the location of Washington in both its hemispheres?

_____

WASHINGTON'S LATITUDE AND LONGITUDE

We also use latitude and longitude lines to help us locate places in Washington. Use your grid skills to locate places within our state!

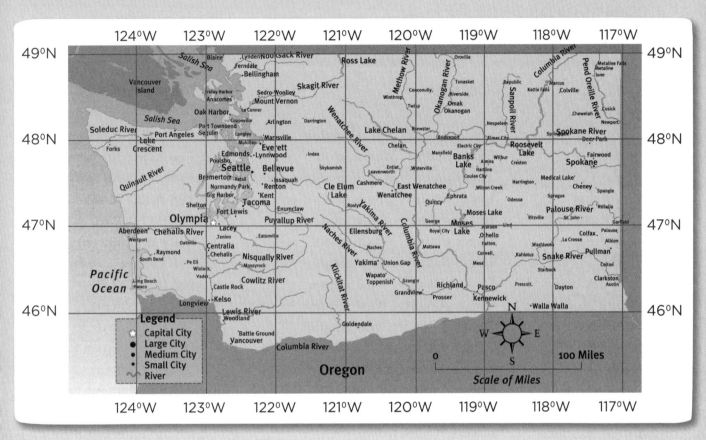

1. Which line of latitude creates the northern border of Washington?

_____

2. Washington's capital city is located between which two lines of latitude?

_____

3. Name one city that is located between 120 degrees west and 119 degrees west.

_____

4. Name one city that is located very near the 123 degrees west line of longitude.

_____

5. Describe the location of Ellensburg.

_____

6. Describe the location of Seattle.

_____

ELEVATION EXPLORATION

This table shows the names and elevations of Washington's mountain ranges. Study the chart and use the information to answer the questions on page 234.

Range	County	Elevation
Bailey Range	Clallam County, Washington	5,627 ft (1,715 m)
Beezley Hills	Grant County, Washington	2,717 ft (828 m)
Black Hills	Thurston County, Washington	2,543 ft (775 m)
Blue Mountains	Union County, Oregon	**9,108 ft (2,776 m)**
Boylston Mountains	Kittitas County, Washington	3,435 ft (1,047 m)
Cascade Range	Pierce County, Washington	**14,409 ft (4,392 m)**
Cedar Hills	King County, Washington	659 ft (201 m)
Chelan Mountains	Chelan County, Washington	6,995 ft (2,132 m)
Chiwaukum Mountains	Chelan County, Washington	6,562 ft (2,000 m)
Coleman Hill	Douglas County, Washington	2,336 ft (712 m)
Columbia Hills	Klickitat County, Washington	2,667 ft (813 m)
Crazy Hills	Skamania County, Washington	4,094 ft (1,248 m)
Cultus Mountains	Skagit County, Washington	4,094 ft (1,248 m)]
Doty Hills	Lewis County, Washington	2,428 ft (740 m)
Elwha River Range	Clallam County, Washington	4,606 ft (1,404 m)
Enchantment Peaks	Chelan County, Washington	8,373 ft (2,552 m)
Entiat Mountains	Chelan County, Washington	5,207 ft (1,587 m)
Frenchman Hills	Grant County, Washington	1,640 ft (500 m)
Green Mountain	Clark County, Washington	1,844 ft (562 m)
Hog Ranch Buttes	Yakima County, Washington	4,206 ft (1,282 m)
Horse Heaven Hills	Benton County, Washington	3,848 ft (1,173 m)
Huckleberry Range	Stevens County, Washington	4,938 ft (1,505 m)
Iron Mountains	Stevens County, Washington	4,632 ft (1,412 m)
Karakul Hills	Adams County, Washington	1,998 ft (609 m)
Kettle River Range	Ferry County, Washington	7,116 ft (2,169 m)
Kruger Mountain	Okanogan County, Washington	2,526 ft (770 m)
Lance Hills	Spokane County, Washington	2,451 ft (747 m)
Lead King Hills	Pend Oreille County, Washington	2,969 ft (905 m)
Monte Cristo Range	Klickitat County, Washington	3,445 ft (1,050 m)
Newcastle Hills	King County, Washington	1,106 ft (337 m)
Olympic Mountains	Jefferson County, Washington	7,962 ft (2,427 m)

Range	County	Elevation
Paradise Hills	Skamania County, Washington	3,714 ft (1,132 m)
Picket Range	Whatcom County, Washington	7,848 ft (2,392 m)
Porter Hills	Pierce County, Washington	**328 ft (100 m)**
Pot Hills	Douglas County, Washington	2,228 ft (679 m)
Quilcene Range	Jefferson County, Washington	3,238 ft (987 m)
Rattlesnake Hills	Yakima County, Washington	2,188 ft (667 m)
Saddle Mountains	Grant County, Washington	2,625 ft (800 m)
Sand Hills	Adams County, Washington	1,450 ft (440 m)
Sand Hills	Ferry County, Washington	1,824 ft (556 m)
Selkirk Mountains	Boundary County, Idaho	5,331 ft (1,625 m)
Sentinel Bluffs	Grant County, Washington	1,388 ft (423 m)
Seven Sisters	Chelan County, Washington	7,185 ft (2,190 m)
Simcoe Mountains	Klickitat County, Washington	3,760 ft (1,150 m)
Skagit Range	Whatcom County, Washington	7,027 ft (2,142 m)
Skyrocket Hills	Walla Walla County, Washington	2,064 ft (629 m)
Sluiskin Mountains	Pierce County, Washington	6,818 ft (2,078 m)
Sophys Meadows	Okanogan County, Washington	4,741 ft (1,445 m)
South Twentymile Meadows	Okanogan County, Washington	5,699 ft (1,737 m)
Stuart Range	Chelan County, Washington	8,067 ft (2,459 m)
Tatoosh Range	Lewis County, Washington	6,063 ft (1,848 m)
The Foothills	Clallam County, Washington	2,447 ft (746 m)
The Summit Range	Stevens County, Washington	3,766 ft (1,148 m)
Three Rocks	Spokane County, Washington	3,612 ft (1,101 m)
Tiffany Meadows	Okanogan County, Washington	6,184 ft (1,885 m)
Toutle Mountain Range	Cowlitz County, Washington	2,726 ft (831 m)
Twin Mountains	Stevens County, Washington	3,258 ft (993 m)
Twin Sisters Range	Whatcom County, Washington	5,548 ft (1,691 m)
Wenatchee Mountains	Chelan County, Washington	5,958 ft (1,816 m)
Westcott Hills	Pierce County, Washington	335 ft (102 m)
White Mountains	Chelan County, Washington	6,722 ft (2,049 m)
Wilkes Hills	Cowlitz County, Washington	551 ft (168 m)
Willapa Hills	Pacific County, Washington	**187 ft (57 m)**

1. What is the elevation of the highest mountain range in feet?

_____

2. What is the elevation of the lowest mountain range in feet?

_____

3. What is the difference in elevation between the highest and lowest mountain ranges?

_____

4. What is the difference in elevation between the highest and the second highest mountain ranges?

_____

5. What is the difference in elevation between the lowest and the second to lowest mountain ranges?

_____

6. In which thousand feet span is the most common mountain range elevation?

_____

7. What is the difference in elevation between the Blue Mountains and the Olympic Mountains?

_____

8. What is the difference in elevation between the Columbia Hills and the Huckleberry range?

_____

9. What is the difference in elevation between the Hog Ranch Buttes and the Paradise Hills?

_____

10. What is the difference in elevation between the highest mountain peak in the United States (Mount McKinley 20,322 feet) and the Cascade Range?

_____

11. What is the difference in elevation between the highest mountain peak in the world (Mount Everest 29,029 feet) and the Cascade Range?

_____

FIELD TRIP: TAKE A HIKE!

There are many beautiful places to hike in Washington! From beach trails to mountain peaks, there are amazing places to explore! This website provides you with a list of the most popular hiking trails in our spectacular state: www.everytrail.com/best/hiking-washington.

With the help of an adult, plan a field trip for your family to enjoy the outdoors. Here are some questions to help you find a great trail.

Would your family prefer an easy, moderate, or difficult hike?

_____

Would you prefer a hike that takes an hour or less, a half-day hike, or a full-day hike?

_____

What type of change in elevation would you like to experience? Would you prefer a gradual climb, a steep climb, or very little change in elevation at all?

_____

Once you've made your decision, answer the following questions. You may need to research several websites to find the answers. Make sure you have an adult's permission before you go online!

Which trail are you going to take?

_____

What is the distance of this trail?

_____

What is the change in elevation of this trail?

_____

How many miles it is away from your house?

_____

How long will it take you to get there?

_____

What supplies will you need to pack?

_____

CREATE A MAP OF YOUR BEDROOM

Use the blank map grid below to make a map of your bedroom. Instead of a scale of miles, a scale of feet or yards will work better for your map. Decide which scale to use and mark the measurements on the scale below. Then estimate how far apart the items in your bedroom are and draw them on the grid.

	A	B	C	D	E	F	G
1							
2							
3							
4							
5							
6							
7							

SCALE

I   J   K   L   M   N   O

LET'S "SEA" SOME SALARIES!

Have you ever considered a career as a football player? If you're a great player who wants to make big bucks, now might be a good time to consider it. Study the salaries of some of the NFL players on the Seattle Seahawks team. Answer the questions about the figures.

PLAYER	NO	POS	AGE	H	W	EXP	SALARY
Russell Okung	76	T	27	6'5"	310	5	$8,760,000
Cliff Avril	56	DE	28	6'3"	260	7	$7,000,000
Marshawn Lynch	24	RB	28	5'11"	215	8	$6,000,000
Brandon Mebane	92	DT	30	6'1"	311	8	$5,500,000
Max Unger	60	C	28	6'5"	305	6	$5,000,000
Kam Chancellor	31	S	26	6'3"	232	5	$4,725,000
Earl Thomas	29	S	25	5'10"	202	5	$4,725,000
Michael Bennett	72	DE	29	6'4"	274	6	$2,000,000
Kevin Williams	94	DT	34	6'5"	311	12	$1,500,000
Demarcus Dobbs	95	DE	27	6'2"	282	4	$1,431,000
Richard Sherman	25	CB	26	6'3"	195	4	$1,431,000
K.J. Wright	50	LB	25	6'4"	246	4	$1,431,000
James Carpenter	77	G	25	6'5"	321	4	$1,417,000
Doug Baldwin	89	WR	26	5'10"	189	4	$1,400,000
Jon Ryan	9	P	33	6'0"	217	9	$1,400,000
Heath Farwell	55	LB	33	6'0"	235	10	$1,250,000
Bruce Irvin	51	LB	27	6'3"	248	3	$1,239,290
Tarvaris Jackson	7	QB	31	6'2"	225	9	$1,100,000
Jeron Johnson	23	S	26	5'10"	212	4	$1,000,000
Tony McDaniel	99	DT	30	6'7"	305	9	$1,000,000
Tony Moeaki	88	TE	27	6'3"	252	5	$1,000,000
Anthony McCoy	85	TE	29	6'5"	259	5	$950,000
Zach Miller	86	TE	29	6'5"	255	8	$900,000
Steven Hauschaka	4	K	29	6'4"	210	7	$875,000

source: http://www.foxsports.com/nfl/seattle-seahawks-team-roster

Who is the highest paid player on the team?

Come up with any combination of salaries of other players that would come close to equaling Russell Okung's salary.

What is the salary difference between the first and second-highest paid players on the team?

Can you draw any conclusions about a correlation between a player's weight and his salary?

What is the total of the salaries of the five highest paid players?

This chart doesn't show all of the players and salaries. However, what is the difference in salary between the highest and lowest paid players on this chart?

FIELD TRIP: SEAHAWKS GAME

Are you a Seahawks fan? Have you ever been to a game? Now that you know so much about the players' salaries, you should go to a game and see what they do to earn their pay! If you can't actually go to a game, watch one on TV.

What team did the Seahawks play against in the game you watched?

_____

What was the final score?

_____

Did the players with the highest salaries play in the game more than those with lower salaries?

_____

Football players are really big guys! Look at the roster from the game (or look it up online) and see if you can figure out who is the tallest player on the team.

_____

Who weighs the most?

_____

Why do you think football players need to be so big and strong?

_____

By looking at the weights of all the players on the roster, what is your best guess for the average weight of the team?

_____

How much do you weigh?

_____

Who weighs more, you or the heaviest player on the team?

_____

Heavier by how much?

_____

COMPUTE THE COMMUTE

Most people in Washington live in or around the biggest cities. Many people live in suburbs outside of the large cities and commute, or drive, to the big cities each day to work. Calculate just how far some of these commuters drive each week.

Sasha and her family live in Bellevue. Her dad works in Seattle. Monday through Friday, he drives from Bellevue to Seattle to work and back again at the end of the day. Each trip in one direction is 11.6 miles. How many miles does Sasha's dad commute each week?

_____

Leah is a nurse and lives in Colbert. She drives to the hospital in Spokane four days a week for work. Each trip in one direction is about 14 miles. How many miles does Leah commute each week?

_____

Diego and his family live in Centralia. His mom works in downtown Tacoma, which is about 58 miles away. She works five days a week. How many miles does Diego's mom commute each week?

_____

Does someone in your family drive to work? How far does he or she travel each day?

_____

How far does he or she travel each week?

_____

SOUNDERS' GOALS

The Seattle Sounders FC Major League Soccer team just played the New England Revolution in an exciting game! The Sounders' GOAL was to WIN! Solve the math problems below. Add up the answers to see who finished on top.

Place the answers from group A on the Sounders' soccer balls and the answers from group B on the Revolution's soccer balls. Then add each column. The team with the highest total "math score" won the game.

A	SOUNDERS	B	REVOLUTION
8 x 8 =	_____	5 x 3 =	_____
40 ÷ 5 =	_____	20 ÷ 4 =	_____
6 x 7 =	_____	6 x 8 =	_____
81 ÷ 9 =	_____	7 ÷ 7 =	_____
3 x 7 =	_____	9 x 3 =	_____
16 ÷ 4 =	_____	100 ÷ 2 =	_____
Total	_____	Total	_____

Who won the game? _____

MARINERS BASEBALL

The Seattle Mariners baseball team is a Major League Baseball team in the Western Division of the American League. Many people in Washington love the game of baseball, and they love to cheer for the Mariners! Find the answers to the math problems below to break the secret code. You'll find out where the Seattle Mariners play.

Add or subtract. Regroup if needed.

I 4,121 + 4,093	T 5,902 + 8,850	A 9,328 + 7,477	B 2,857 + 8,149	E 7,529 + 9,342
P 8,939 - 826	D 4,824 - 3,912	K 5,670 - 3,333	C 10,296 - 3, 053	S 8,642 - 2, 468
L 3,573 + 5,441	R 4,805 - 2,604	N 1,999 + 6,529	O 7,461 - 5,509	F 429 - 421

THE MARINERS PLAY THEIR GAMES: _____ _____   _____
                                   16,805 14,752   16,805

_____ _____ _____ _____ _____ _____ _____ _____
11,006 16,805 9,014   9,014   8,113   16,805 2,201   2,337

_____ _____ _____ _____ _____ _____
7,243   16,805 9,014   9,014   16,871 912

_____ _____ _____ _____ _____ _____
6,174   16,805   8   16,871 7,243   1,952

_____ _____ _____ _____ _____
  8   8,214   16,871 9,014   912

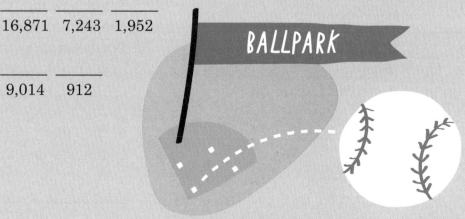

BALLPARK

THE FIRST PEOPLE

The first people to live in the area we know as Washington were American Indians. This timeline shows when different groups of American Indians lived in Washington. Use the information from the timeline to answer questions.

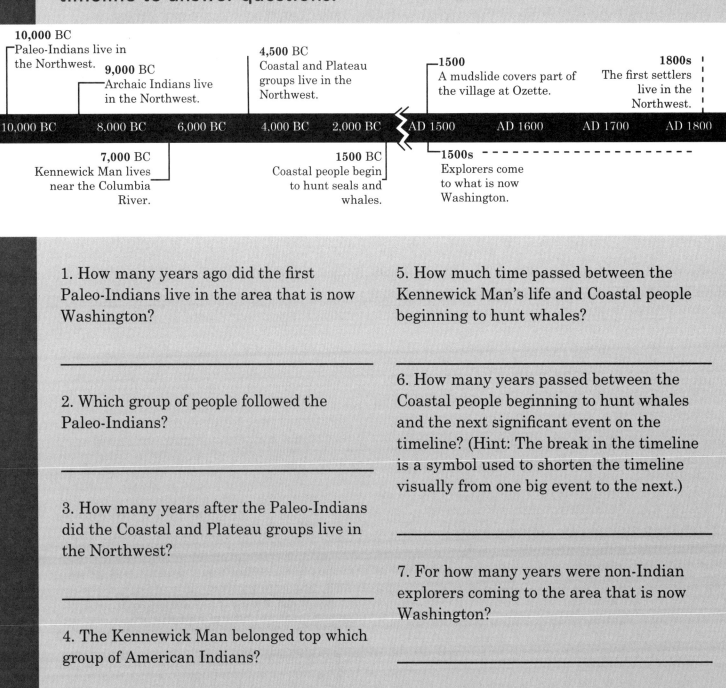

10,000 BC — Paleo-Indians live in the Northwest.

9,000 BC — Archaic Indians live in the Northwest.

4,500 BC — Coastal and Plateau groups live in the Northwest.

1500 — A mudslide covers part of the village at Ozette.

1800s — The first settlers live in the Northwest.

7,000 BC — Kennewick Man lives near the Columbia River.

1500 BC — Coastal people begin to hunt seals and whales.

1500s — Explorers come to what is now Washington.

Timeline axis: 10,000 BC | 8,000 BC | 6,000 BC | 4,000 BC | 2,000 BC | AD 1500 | AD 1600 | AD 1700 | AD 1800

1. How many years ago did the first Paleo-Indians live in the area that is now Washington?

_____

2. Which group of people followed the Paleo-Indians?

_____

3. How many years after the Paleo-Indians did the Coastal and Plateau groups live in the Northwest?

_____

4. The Kennewick Man belonged top which group of American Indians?

_____

5. How much time passed between the Kennewick Man's life and Coastal people beginning to hunt whales?

_____

6. How many years passed between the Coastal people beginning to hunt whales and the next significant event on the timeline? (Hint: The break in the timeline is a symbol used to shorten the timeline visually from one big event to the next.)

_____

7. For how many years were non-Indian explorers coming to the area that is now Washington?

_____

8. How many years ago did the first non-Indian settlers live in the Northwest?

_____

HOW FAR IS A MILE?

The first people who lived in Washington did a lot of walking. They likely walked a mile or more each day to hunt or gather food. They walked everywhere they went! Can you imagine if you had to walk everywhere you went—to get to school, to buy groceries, to see the doctor, or to visit a family member?

Have you ever walked or ran a mile? It can feel like a very long distance. A mile is 5,280 feet. How many yards are in a mile? You can convert the length from feet to yards as long as you know how many feet are in a yard.

> THERE ARE _____ FEET IN A YARD.

Now, we need to see how many groups of three feet are in the total 5,280 feet of a mile. When we talk about "groups of" we are either using multiplication or division. Since we know we are looking for an amount smaller than 5,280, we are using division.

> 5,280 FEET ÷ _____ FEET = _____ YARDS (THE NUMBER OF YARDS IN A MILE)

Now it's time to walk the walk! Walk or run a mile with a family member. Talk to them about what it would be like if you had to walk everywhere you went.

UNDERSTAND DATES AND TIMELINES

Historians use many terms to describe different periods of time. Understanding these terms will help you learn more about when significant events took place in Washington's history.

A DECADE IS 10 YEARS

A CENTURY IS 100 YEARS

AN ERA IS A PERIOD OF YEARS WHEN RELATED EVENTS HAPPENED. THERE IS NO SPECIFIC AMOUNT OF TIME.

1. How many decades make up a century?

_____

2. How many years are in a half-century?

_____

3. How many decades are in a half-century?

_____

4. How many years are in three-quarters of a century?

_____

5. How many decades are in three-quarters of a century?

_____

6. About how many decades old are you? Round to the nearest decade. (Example: If you are 12, you are about 1 decade old.)

_____

7. About how many decades old are your parents?

_____

8. If the United States became a country in 1776, how many centuries old is our country? Round to the nearest half-century.

_____

9. If Paleo-Indians lived in the Northwest beginning in 10,000 BC, about how many centuries ago was that? About how many decades ago was that?

_____

10. If Coastal people began to hunt seals and whales in 1500 BC, about how many centuries ago was that?

_____

About how many decades ago was that?

_____

MATH FOR THE JOURNEY WEST

When travelers came west on the Oregon Trail, they had to pack plenty of food and supplies for the long, hard journey. Here are some recommendations of what to pack for a family of four. Use the information to help you calculate some of the numbers needed to pack the correct items.

SUPPLIES

Recommendations:
• Wagon 4 x 10 feet (built to hold about 2,000 pounds of supplies)
• 4 to 6 oxen, cattle, or horses

Food for a family of four:
• 200 pounds of flour
• 100 pounds of beans
• 100 pounds of lard
• 150 pounds of bacon
• 10 pounds of coffee
• 20 pounds of sugar
• 10 pounds of salt

How much flour would be needed for a family of six?

_____

If divided equally, how many pounds of beans was each member of the family of four given for the journey?

_____

If a family used two pounds of flour a day, how many days would 200 pounds of flour last?

_____

On average, pioneers were able to travel about 12 miles per day. At this rate, about how many days would it take them to travel the 2,000 miles of the Oregon Trail?

_____

This list was recommended for a family of four. Figure out how much of each item you would need to pack for your family. What other food supplies would you take? Would you exchange any of the items on the list for other items? Write your family's supply list on another piece of paper.

ALONG THE NEZ PERCE TRAIL

The Nez Perce Indians were a large historic tribe living in the area that is now known as Washington. The Nez Perce were forced off their land because the U.S. government wanted valuable resources from the land. Chief Joseph, the leader of the Nez Perce tribe, led his people in an escape toward Canada. The U.S. army followed them, and there were many battles. In the end, Chief Joseph had to surrender to the U.S. army because his people had run out of supplies, the weather turned cold, and many people were sick or wounded. This map shows the trail the Nez Perce followed toward Canada. Study the map and answer the questions.

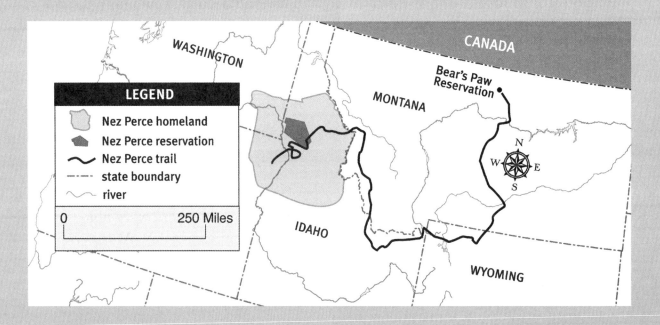

What is this a map of?

_____

About how many miles wide was the Nez Perce **homeland** from east to west?

_____

About how many miles wide was the Nez Perce **reservation** from east to west?

_____

Estimate the length of the Nez Perce Trail.

_____

About how many miles from Canada is the Bear Paw Battlefield?

_____

RAILROADS BRING CHANGE

In 1883, the railroads came to Washington. With them came many changes. Now, it was much easier for people to visit our state and even move to the area from other places. Look at these numbers that show how three of Washington's cities grew in just ten years because of the railroads.

CITY	SEATTLE	TACOMA	SPOKANE
Population in 1880	3,533	1,098	350
Population in 1890	42,837	36,006	19,992

By how much did the population of each town grow from 1880 to 1890?

_____

_____

_____

Which town was the largest in 1880? And in 1890?

_____

Which town was the smallest in 1880? And in 1890?

_____

If you had to make a prediction about the growth patterns of these cities after 1890, what would your prediction be? Why?

_____

_____

_____

Being a dedicated student and learning and challenging your brain to get stronger are great ways to prepare for adulthood and the working world. Give your brain a math workout with this teaser!

Try to fill in the missing numbers.
The missing numbers are integers between 2 and 15.
The numbers in each row add up to totals to the right.
The numbers in each column add up to the totals along the bottom.
The diagonal lines also add up the totals to the right.

					30
6		7	2		21
3		6	3	6	28
4		9		6	35
10	14		7	6	49
	12	9	5	3	31
25	45	43	28	23	35

EMPLOYMENT IN WASHINGTON

This chart shows how many people work in Washington's major industries.

INDUSTRY	NUMBER OF EMPLOYEES (MARCH 2013)
TRADE, TRANSPORTATION, AND UTILITIES	548,200
GOVERNMENT	540,900
EDUCATION AND HEALTH SERVICES	392,200
PROFESSIONAL AND BUSINESS SERVICES	352,000
MANUFACTURING	288,000
LEISURE AND HOSPITALITY	281,700
FINANCIAL ACTIVITIES	142,300
OTHER SERVICES	112,400
INFORMATION	104,700
MINING, LOGGING, AND CONSTRUCTION	6,100

1. What is shown on this chart?

_____

2. Which industry has the most employees?

_____

3. Which industry has the fewest employees?

_____

4. What is the difference in number of employees between the largest and smallest industries?

_____

5. Which two industries have the two closest numbers of employees?

_____

6. How many employees total are represented by this graph?

_____

WASHINGTON'S TOP 10 EXPORTS

This graph shows the top ten items that Washington makes or grows and sells to other countries.

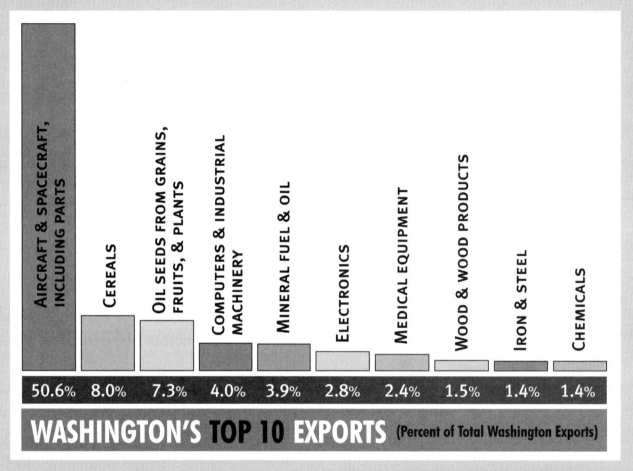

AIRCRAFT & SPACECRAFT, INCLUDING PARTS	CEREALS	OIL SEEDS FROM GRAINS, FRUITS, & PLANTS	COMPUTERS & INDUSTRIAL MACHINERY	MINERAL FUEL & OIL	ELECTRONICS	MEDICAL EQUIPMENT	WOOD & WOOD PRODUCTS	IRON & STEEL	CHEMICALS
50.6%	8.0%	7.3%	4.0%	3.9%	2.8%	2.4%	1.5%	1.4%	1.4%

WASHINGTON'S TOP 10 EXPORTS (Percent of Total Washington Exports)

Source: World Institute for Strategic Economic Research and U.S. Census Bureau Foreign Trade Division

1. What is Washington's number one export?

_____

2. What is the percentage difference between the top two exports?

_____

3. Would you say that Washington's top two exports have about the same number of exports? Why or why not?

_____

4. What percentage of Washington's exports do food-related products make up?

_____

5. What percentage of Washington's exports relies on Washington's trees?

_____

6. How many industries' percentages combined would it take to equal a percentage close to the top export's percentage?

_____

WASHINGTON'S TOP 10 TRADING PARTNERS FOR EXPORTS

This graph shows the top ten countries to which Washington exports products.

1. Which country is Washington's number one trading partner?

_____

2. What percentage of Washington's exports go to China?

_____

3. Which country is Washington's number two trading partner?

_____

4. What percentage of Washington's exports go to Canada?

_____

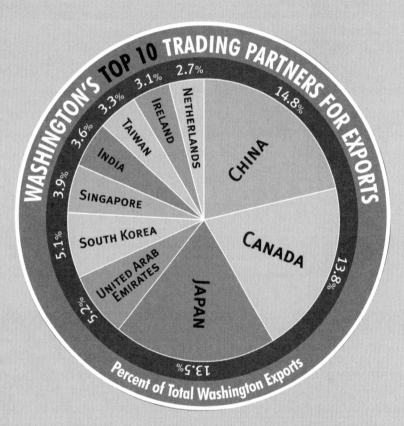

5. What country is Washington's number three trading partner?

_____

6. What percentage of Washington's exports go to Japan?

_____

7. Would you say that Washington's top three export countries receive about the same amount of exports from Washington? Why or why not?

_____

8. Which of the top ten trading partners receives the fewest exports from Washington?

_____

9. What total percentage of Washington's exports go to Asian countries?

_____

10. What total percentage of Washington's exports go to Western European countries?

STATE SYMBOLS

Bird:
Willow Goldfinch

In 1928, government leaders let school children choose the state bird. The meadowlark won, but it was already the state bird for seven other states. A few years later, women in the state voted for the goldfinch, and for a while there were two state birds. In 1951, children again voted, and the goldfinch became the official state bird.

Flower:
Coast Rhododendron

Washington women voted on the state flower in 1883. Six flowers were considered, but the final decision was between clover and the "rhodie."

Tree:
Western Hemlock

At first, Washington newspapers chose the western red cedar as the state tree. They picked it because it was so important to early Native Americans. Other people said the hemlock "would become the backbone of this state's forest industry." The hemlock was made the official state tree in 1947.

Insect:
Green Darner Dragonfly

In 1997, the dragonfly became our state insect after elementary students in Kent brought the idea to the legislature. Students all over the state voted for a state insect. Also known as the "mosquito hawk," the dragonfly eats large numbers of pesky mosquitoes and other insects. It has a 4-inch wingspan and can fly over 25 miles per hour.

Fish:
Steelhead Trout
Steelhead trout is one of the most popular fish for sport fishing. This amazing creature returns to lay eggs at the same place where it began life. It became our state fish in 1969.

Fruit:
Apple
Washington is famous for its apples. During World War II, dried apples were shipped to soldiers overseas. When the war ended, Washington farmers had too many apples. They started making frozen apple juice and apple candy. They started growing different kinds of apples to sell. In 1989, 100 years after statehood, the apple became a state symbol.

Dance:
Square Dance
When pioneers came west, they brought a dance called the quadrille, which means "square" in French. Dancers are directed by a caller. They turn and move to the tune of fiddle music.

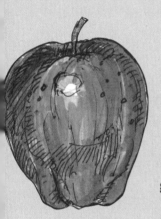

Fossil:
Columbian Mammoth
In 1998, students near Cheney led the effort to make the mammoth our state fossil. Mammoths ate grasses and other plants. Males were about the size of modern elephants, and females were smaller. Nearly all mammoths died out about 10,000 years ago.

Flag:
Washington's state flag is the only state flag that is green. It is also the only state flag with a picture of a president on it. The state flag has the state seal in the center. The words "The Seal of the State of Washington, 1889" were written around the seal. What happened in 1889?

GLOSSARY

A

agreement: when both sides agree on what to do

agriculture: the business of raising crops and animals to sell

ancient: relating to a time long, long ago

archaeologist: a scientist who studies clues to learn how people lived in the past

artifact: an object made or used by people of the past

atlatl: a tool used to throw a spear farther and faster

autobiography: a book written by a person about his or her own life

B

barter: to trade without using money

belief: something thought to be true

benefit: what you get in return for paying the cost

bill: a written proposal for a law

biography: the story of a person's life as written by another person

brigade: a large group of trappers or soldiers organized for a special activity

C

cargo: goods carried on a ship, train, truck, or plane

century: a time period of 100 years

ceremony: a ritual; actions done the same way each time for a special purpose

chronological: arranged in the order of time

citizen: a legal resident of a country

civic: having to do with being a citizen of a city or town

civilize: to bring to a higher stage of education and culture

claim: to take as a rightful owner

climate: the weather pattern year after year

community: a group of people living near each other in a place

compass: a symbol that shows direction on a map (north, south, east, west)

compromise: an agreement that is reached by each side giving up something it wants

conflict: a problem between two people or groups

conserve: to protect or save something for the future

constitution: a written plan for government

consumer: any person who buys goods and services

continent: one of the Earth's seven large land areas that are almost completely surrounded by water

convert: to change another person's religious beliefs

cost: what you give up to get what you want

council: a meeting where a group of people makes decisions

country: a land region under the control of one government

county: a government region within a state

cultural characteristic: a feature that has to do with the way people live

D

decade: a time period of 10 years

defend: to drive away danger or attack

descendant: children, grandchildren, great-grandchildren, and so on

discrimination: to treat other people badly just because they are different

disease: sickness

distributor: a person or company that transports goods to market

document: an official government paper

duty: an action a person is expected to do

E

economics: the study of how people produce, sell, and buy goods and services

elder: an older person

election: the process of voting people into a government office

elevation: how high the land is above the level of the ocean

encounter: to meet face to face

enforce: to make sure people obey (a law or rule)

era: a period of years when related events happened

ethnic: referring to a minority race

expedition: a journey taken for a specific purpose

explore: to travel to a new place to learn about it

export: to ship goods or services out to other countries

extinct: no longer living anywhere on the Earth

F

felt: a thick cloth made by pressing and heating fur and wool together

fertile: good for growing crops

frontier: a region on the edge of settled land

fur trade: a business where animal fur is traded for other things or for money

G

gateway: an opening; a way to enter a place

geography: the study of the Earth and the people, animals, and plants living on it

global: relating to the whole world

gold rush: a rush to a new gold field in hopes of getting rich

goods: things that are made and then bought and sold

governor: the top government leader of a territory or state

H

hardship: suffering

harpoon: a long spear used to hunt whales

historian: a person who studies many sources to learn about events of the past

history: the story of the past

homestead: to claim, farm, and improve land

hydroelectricity: electricity produced by water power

I

ideal: an idea about the way things should be; something that is believed to be perfect or best

immigrant: a person who moves into a country

immigrate: to move into a new country or place to live

import: to bring goods or services into a country from another country

industry: a certain kind of business, such as manufacturing, shipping, tourism, etc.

interpreter: one who translates one language into another as someone is talking

irrigation: bringing water to crops from a river or lake

L

labor: workers; working

landform: a natural feature of the land

legend: (1) on a map, a key to the meaning of symbols; (2) story that tells about the past or how things came to be

liberty: freedom; the state of being free

livestock: animals raised for food, such as cows, chickens, turkey, sheep, and hogs

longhouse: long Indian homes where several families lived together

lumber: logs sawed into boards

M

massacre: the violent murder of a large group of people

missionary: a person who tries to teach his or her religion to others

N

native: being born or raised in a certain place or region

natural boundary: a boundary line formed by natural landforms, such as rivers or mountain ranges

natural resource: something found in nature that people use, such as trees, water, or minerals

negotiate: to talk back and forth to reach an agreement

O

opportunity: a good chance for progress or advancement

oral history: a story told aloud and passed down from person to person

orphanage: a home for children who have no parents

overland: across land

ownership: the fact of being an owner

P

pelt: the skin of an animal with the fur still attached

perspective: point of view

petroglyph: a rock carving

physical characteristic: a feature that has to do with the natural land and landforms

pioneer: a person who is among the first settlers to move to a new place

point of view: the way a person sees an event

political boundary: a boundary line decided by people

politics: having to do with government

population: all the people who live in a particular area

portrait: a picture of a person in words, art, or a photograph

potlatch: a ceremony of feasting and gift-giving

primary source: an object or writing made by a person who was there at the time

processed: made in a factory; having gone through changes to produce or manufacture something

producer: a person or company that makes, grows, or supplies goods for sale

product: something that is made to sell

profitable: able to make money

R

rapids: a part of the river where the current is fast and large boulders stick out of the water

region: a land division based on common characteristics

religion: relating to beliefs, practices, and worship of God or the supernatural

representative: a person elected to vote for other people

reservation: land set aside for Native Americans

reservoir: a large lake used as a source of water

responsibility: a duty you have to do; something you are supposed to do

rights: the privileges citizens are entitled to

rule of law: the idea that no one is above the law; the law is the highest power

rural: having to do with the countryside rather than a town or city

S

sawmill: a building where logs are sawed into boards

scale: compares distance on a map to actual distance on land

secondary source: information made later, after an event has happened

services: in economics, people who work for other people for money

shaman: a spiritual leader who tried to heal the sick

slave: a person owned by another

slavery: people who are bought and sold and forced to work

sovereignty: self-rule; supreme power or authority

spike: a very long, thick nail

spiritual: having to do with the spirit life and not the physical

state: a part of a country that makes some of its own laws; a political region of a country

stockade: a strong, tall fence made from logs

surrender: to give up

survey: to measure the land

sustain: to support or strengthen

symbol: a mark or design that stands for something else

T

tax: money people must pay to the government

technology: the use of scientific knowledge

terrain: a piece of land; ground

territory: a land region owned and ruled by a country; a region that is not a state

timber: wood (from trees) that is used for building

trade route: a route of travel over water or land that is used by traders

tradition: a way of doing something the same way your ancestors did it

tragedy: a horrible event

treaty: a written agreement between two groups

trek: an organized journey of a group of people

tribal council: a group that makes laws for an Indian tribe on Indian lands

tule: tall plants or reeds that grow wild in swampy places

tourism: the industry of making money by meeting the needs of visitors

U-W

urban: having to do with a city

veto: to say no to a bill; to prevent a bill from becoming a law

volunteer: a person who chooses to work without pay

wagon train: a large group of wagons that followed each other

weir: a fence built across a stream to catch fish

wilderness: a place in its natural state, where few people live

ANSWER KEY

VOCABULARY

Find the Hidden Message! (page 10)

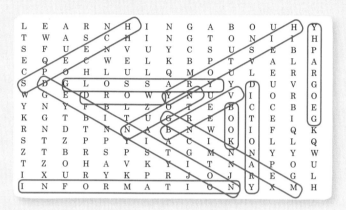

Tools of History (page 14)

1. G
2. C
3. H
4. F
5. I
6. B
7. E
8. D
9. A

Fill in the Blank (page 15)

1. Century
2. Chronological
3. Decade
4. Document
5. Era
6. Historian
7. Point of view
8. Primary source
9. Secondary source

Where in the World Are We? (page 16)

1. world
2. continent
3. country, Canada, Mexico
4. state, Oregon, Idaho

Hike the Maze (page 20)

Land Regions (page 22)

1. agricultural
2. industries
3. no change/student sentence
4. regions
5. no change/student sentence
6. tourist, touring

The First People (page 24)

1. native
2. archeologist
3. petroglyph
4. ancient
5. descendants
6. extinct
7. atlatl

Coastal People (page 28)

Across	Down
3. harpoon	1. ceremony
5. legend	2. potlatch
6. tradition	4. weir

Plateau People (page 30)

1. spiritual
2. barter
3. tule
4. belief
5. shaman
6. longhouse
7. elder

1. missionaries
2. religion
3. convert
4. disease
5. tragedy
6. massacre
7. orphanage

Explore the Crossword (page 33)

Across

3. encounter
5. claim
6. fur trade

Down

1. trade route
2. pelt
4. explore

The Oregon Trail (page 41)

1. slavery
2. benefit
3. homestead
4. immigrant
5. cost
6. hardship
7. frontier
8. pioneer

Exploring by Sea (page 34)

Spain
England
United States
Sea

Exploring by Land (page 36)

1. overland
2. slave
3. expedition
4. interpreter
5. terrain
6. rapids

Trail Maze (page 43)

The Missionaries (page 39)

N	I	A	R	R	E	T	D	O	V	E	R	A	N	D
O	E	P	N	N	O	S	D	N	A	L	R	E	V	O
S	S	R	N	E	A	T	T	I	D	E	P	X	E	V
L	S	E	X	E	D	I	T	I	O	N	I	P	D	I
A	D	P	I	N	T	E	R	P	R	E	T	E	R	R
V	I	I	E	L	V	D	T	E	R	R	A	I	T	I
I	P	D	I	A	P	S	L	N	T	L	R	E	V	O
R	A	S	L	A	I	N	T	E	R	P	E	T	E	R
I	R	S	R	E	X	P	E	D	I	T	I	O	N	D
V	E	E	R	D	S	I	P	P	X	A	V	R	N	S

Two New Territories (page 44)

1. D
2. E
3. C
4. A
5. B
6. F

The Treaty-Making Era (page 46)

Across

4. profitable
7. conflict
8. fertile
9. defend
10. surrender

Down

1. perspective
3. council
5. reservation
6. lumber

Levels of Government (page 50)

1. sovereignty
2. tax
3. constitution
4. representative
5. county
6. tribal council
7. enforce

Our Rights, Our Laws (page 52)

1. rights
2. liberty
3. bill
4. rule of law
5. ideal
6. veto

Legal-Eagle Word Search (page 53)

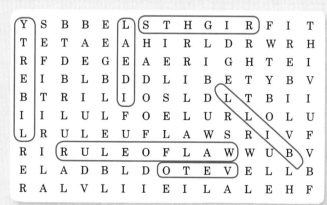

Law Scramble (page 54)

Everyone must obey the law. That's how things stay fair.

The Elements of Our Economy (page 60)

Across

3. economics
4. goods
5. hydroelectricity
7. reservoir
8. sustain

Down

1. labor
2. conserve
6. services

Global Trade (page 66)

1. E
2. D
3. A
4. C
5. B

GEOGRAPHY & SOCIAL STUDIES

Reading and Creating a Timeline (page 72)

1. 2010; five years old
2. He started kindergarten
3. Eleven years; One year for each year since he was born

Hemispheres (page 78)

top left: northern hemisphere
bottom left: southern hemisphere
right: western hemisphere

Map Terms Word Search (page 83)

```
J Z Q U P B D S C A L E O F M I L E S H
P U N W S R B E P H E Q Z J N D Z V E B
L E G E N D I D O O P K N B I Q M M C M
T W T O H M N M E U D J W F N S M C Z X
E Q U A T O R H C M H L R Z P M N X G Y
K H A F L K Q X X L E N Q H T W G M G K
W F U B K I G M X U K R E T F R O E O
E Q J Z Z F V G R D J R I V M S D E J M
U U C O R R V H Z T E Y I D B G A R S J
Z U A V N H X E E T S O O G I V T E U H
O D C L Z E F P M H J Z W O L A D P F I
J J T P D S Y I E H R I C V Z M N K Y W
J H S R G F Q D C G F R Z D B U W F A R
N H H U W J Q T X S P I F Z O G L P S X
O T T C Y E F J S H E C F G B D E E U R
R S U U C J I Q G C O M P A S S R O S E
T E Y T O K A O I N O V F Y A G R R Z F
H W L W C S X P W W U Q V W D P F F V Q
B B L U U M P A W N O Z X W D T Q V Z
```

A Map by Any Other Name . . . Would Still Be a Map (page 86)

1. It tells us how to recognize the sizes of Washington's cities and towns. It also shows us how to find rivers.
2. The title should include something about Washington and its cities and towns.
3. Olympia

Population Map of Washington (page 90)

1. The darker the color, the higher the population. The lighter the color, the lower the population.
2. King County
3. Most of the counties with the highest populations surround the Puget Sound area.
4. Most of the counties with the lowest populations are in the northeast corner of the state, bordering Idaho and Canada.
5. King, Pierce, and Snohomish Counties
6. Answers may include Okanogan, Ferry, Stevens, Pend Oreille, Douglas, Lincoln, Kittitas, Adams, Whitman, Columbia, Garfield, Asotin, Klickitat, Skamania, Wahkiakum, Pacific, Jefferson, and San Juan Counties.
7. Answers may be related to the jobs available in connection with the water, such as shipping and fishing. Answers may also be related to the moderate or mild climate near the coast.
8. Answers will vary.

Important Places in Washington (page 92)

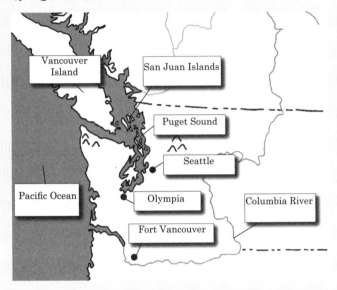

Land Features Crossword Puzzle (page 93)

Across

6. plateaus
8. peninsula

Down

1. mountains
2. inlets
3. cape
4. wetlands
5. island
7. harbor

Land Features (page 94)

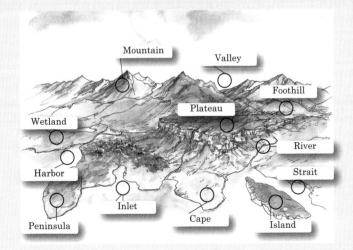

Relief Map (page 96)

1. The areas with lower elevations are green. The higher the elevation, the lighter the green gets until it eventually turns into tan and then brown.
2. Dark green
3. Dark tan/brown
4. Along the coastline
5. Along the Cascade Mountain range, running up and down the state just in from the coast

Indian Tribal Lands (page 116)

1. Yakama and Colville Tribes
2. Most are located in the western half of the state, with many along the coast and in the Puget Sound area.
3. It may have something to do with their way of life; some may be fishermen, whalers, or depend on other natural resources provided by the water. The moderate climates near the coast may also appeal to the tribes.
4. The Colville and Yakama tribes have different natural resources available to them, so they probably eat different foods, live in different kinds of homes, and experience different kinds of weather.
5. Answers will vary.

Lewis and Clark's Journey (page 119)

1. In St. Louis
2. The Missouri River and the Columbia River
3. There are few, if any, mountains where they traveled by river.
4. The area traveled by horse is very mountainous and where many Indian groups lived.
5. Somewhere near the border of present day Washington and Oregon
6. Answers will vary, but may related to weather, wild animals, problems with rivers, and problems with other elements of nature

Lewis and Clark Timeline (page 120)

May 14, 1804
About five months
The men killed a grizzly bear.
The Shoshone
Sacagawea discovered her brother.
October 16, 1805
Dogs
Cloudy and foggy

Fact or Fiction? (page 122)

True
False; their wives and families often traveled with them
True
True
False; most died of old age
False; trapping was a business, and mountain men made money doing it
False; while some were brave, creative, and hardworking, some were also greedy, violent, and racist
True
True

Comparing Maps (page 123)

1. Washington Territory and Oregon Territory
2. A large piece of land in the east of the territory was removed and became part of the Idaho Territory.
3. A large piece of land in the east of the territory was removed and became part of the Idaho Territory and Nebraska Territory.
4. Washington Territory, Oregon Territory, Idaho Territory, Nebraska Territory
5. All the borders are the same except for the eastern borders.

The Pig War (page 124)

1. The San Juan Islands during the pig war and the proposed ways to divide the land.
2. The boundary through the Haro Strait included all of the San Juan Islands as part of the United States of America.

Find the Hidden Term (page 126)

Willow Goldfinch

Western Hemlock

Green Darner Dragonfly

Coast Rhododendron

Steelhead Trout

Apple

Square Dance

Columbian Mammoth

Hidden term: State Symbols

READING AND WRITING

Cite Text Evidence: Mt. Saint Helens (page 154)

In paragraph two, it says there were signs of danger on Mt. Saint Helens. There were small earthquakes and smoke rose from the mountaintop.

In paragraph 3, it says that rocks broke into fine ash. A fountain of ash shot nine miles into the sky and across the state, turning the day into night.

In paragraph 4, it says that the eruption caused mudslides that caused even more damage.

In paragraph 1, it says that some of the mountains are actually volcanoes.

Pacific Rim (page 156)

Lines 1, 2, and 3; The Pacific Rim is a region on the globe that is made up of all the countries that touch the Pacific Ocean.

Lines 4 and 5; Japan, China, Korea, and the United States

Lines 10–13; The countries along the Pacific Rim are able to easily buy and sell goods from one another, which is important for many people to earn a living.

Possible answers include statements about the coastlines and business in the Pacific Rim being affected by hurricanes, tsunamis, or other natural disasters common to coasts. There are many other possibilities related to the ease of travel and close proximity of the countries in the Pacific Rim.

Archaic Tools (page 158)

1. C
2. B
3. C
4. D

Legends (page 162)

Two animals, a coyote and a large bird

The Great Makah Word Hunt (page 166)

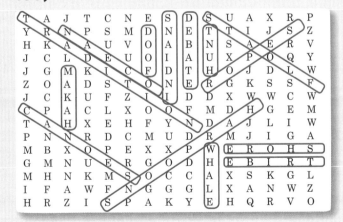

Fur Trade Maze (page 177)

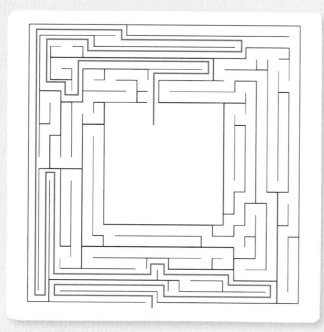

Campfires (page 183)

The first response should mention something about how people settled near places John C. Fremont had camped. Responses to the second question will vary but could mention how Native Americans probably disliked the changes but settlers, miners, explorers, and pioneers probably liked the changes.

SCIENCE

A Climo-What? (page 194)

1. Red
2. Blue
3. Ten degrees
4. With blue bars
5. Late summer months, July and August
6. Winter months, December and January
7. The temperatures rise in the summer months as the amounts of precipitation decrease.
8. The low temperatures follow the same patterns as the high temperatures.
9. There is more precipitation in the colder months.
10. Answers will vary.

Wonderful Water (page 196)

1. evaporation
2. condensation
3. precipitation
4. collection

Inside a Volcano (page 204)

1. Ash cloud
2. Vent
3. Ash
4. Lava Flow
5. Side Vent
6. Flank
7. Sill
8. Branch pipe
9. Layers
10. Rock Layers
11. Pipe
12. Magma Chamber

The Rock Cycle (page 206)

1. Igneous
2. Sedimentary
3. Metamorphic

From Weathered Rocks to Soils (page 214)

1. Plants are the organic matter, and they grow in the topsoil.
2. The larger materials are at the bottom of the soil profile. They are heavier, so they sink to the bottom, while the lighter materials stay on top.
3. The topsoil and organic matter are darkest. The topsoil contains the most dead material, nutrients, and water.

Worm Maze (page 219)

It's in the Dirt Word Search (page 220)

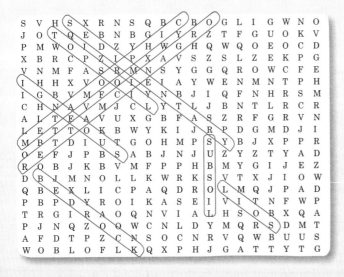

MATH

The Largest Grid in the World (page 230)

1. 45 degrees north
2. South America and Africa
3. Europe and Africa
4. North America
5. the northern hemisphere
6. the southern hemisphere

7. northern
8. western
9. Washington is located in the northwestern hemisphere

Washington's Latitude and Longitude (page 231)

1. 49 degrees north
2. 47 degrees north and 48 degrees north
3. several choices
4. several choices
5. Ellensburg is located between120 and 121 degrees west and on the 47 degrees north line of latitude.
6. Seattle is located 122 and 123 degrees west and between 47 and 48 degrees north.

Elevation Exploration (page 232)

1. 14,409 feet
2. 187 feet
3. 14,222 feet
4. 5,301 feet
5. 141 feet
6. In the 2,000 feet range
7. 1,146 feet
8. 2,271 feet
9. 492 feet
10. 5,913 feet
11. 14,620 feet

Let's "Sea" Some Salaries (page 238)

1. Russell Okung
2. $1,760,000
3. $32,260,000
4. Answer will vary. One possible answer could be the sum of Tony McDaniel's, Jeron Johnson's, Taravris Jackson's, Bruce Irvin's, Heath Farwell's, Jon Ryan's, and Doug Baldwin's salaries, totaling $8,389,290.
5. Although it isn't the case with every player, most of the higher paid players have higher weights.
6. $7,885,000

Compute the Commute (page 241)

116 miles

112 miles

580 miles

Answers will vary.

Sounders' Goals (page 242)

A. 64; 8; 42; 9; 21; 4

B. 15; 5; 48; 1; 27; 50

Sounders' total: 148

Revolution's total: 146

Sounders win!

Mariners Baseball (page 243)

I. 8,214

T. 14,752

A. 16,805

B. 11,006

E. 16,871

P. 8,113

D. 912

K. 2,337

C. 7,243

S. 6,174

L. 9,014

R. 2,201

N. 8,528

O. 1,952

F. 8

The Mariners play their games at a ballpark called Safeco Field.

The First People (page 244)

1. About 12,015 years ago

2. Archaic Indians

3. 5,500 years

4. Archaic Indians

5. 5,500 years

6. 3,000 years

7. 300 years

8. From the year 2015, 215 years; add an additional year for each year after 2015

How Far is a Mile? (page 245)

1. There are three feet in a yard.

2. 5,280 feet ÷ 3 feet = 1,760 yards in a mile.

Understand Dates and Timelines (page 246)

1. 10

2. 50

3. 5

4. 75

5. 7.5

6. Answers will vary.

7. Answers will vary.

8. Almost two and a half centuries old.

9. About 120.15 centuries ago; about 1,201.5 decades

10. About 35.15 centuries ago; about 351.5 decades

Math for the Journey West (page 247)

300 pounds

25 pounds

100 days

About 167 days

Along the Nez Perce Trail (page 248)

The trail the Nez Perce followed towards Canada

About 185 miles

Less than half the width of their homelands

About 1,170 miles long

About 40 miles

Railroads Bring Change (page 249)

Seattle: 39,304; Tacoma: 34,908; Spokane: 19,642

Seattle

Spokane

Brain Teaser Solution (page 250)

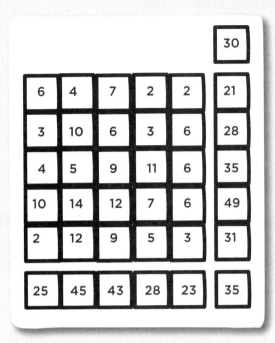

					30
6	4	7	2	2	21
3	10	6	3	6	28
4	5	9	11	6	35
10	14	12	7	6	49
2	12	9	5	3	31
25	45	43	28	23	35

Employment in Washington (page 251)

1. The number of people who work in different industries in Washington
2. Trade, transportation, and utilities
3. Mining, logging, and construction
4. 542,100
5. Manufacturing and leisure and hospitality
6. 2,768,500

Washington's Top 10 Exports (page 252)

1. Aircraft and spacecraft, including parts
2. 42.6%
3. No, there is a 42.6% difference in the amount of exports between the top two exports.
4. Cereals, oil seeds from grains, fruits, and plants make up 15.3% of Washington's exports.
5. Wood and wood products 1.5%
6. All other nine exports, totaling only 32.7%

Washington's Top 10 Trading Partners for Exports (page 253)

1. China
2. 14.8%
3. Canada
4. 13.8%
5. Japan
6. 13.5 %
7. Yes, there is only a 1% and 1.3% difference in the amount of Washington's exports that go to the top three countries.
8. Netherlands
9. Exports to China, Japan, United Arab Emirates, South Korea, Singapore, India, and Taiwan make up 49.4% of Washington's exports.
10. Exports to Ireland and Netherlands make up 5.8% of Washington's exports.